796.324 SHE

THE
Learning
CENTRE

01209 616259
http://webopac.cornwall.ac.uk

Cornwall College Camborne
Learning Centre - FE

This resource is to be returned on or before the last date
stamped below. To renew items please contact the Centre

Three Week Loan

0 9 DEC 2016		

y

ll

lls

11

Also available from Bloomsbury

101 Youth Football Drills – Age 7–11
3rd edition
Malcolm Cook

101 Youth Football Drills – Age 12–16
3rd edition
Malcolm Cook

101 Youth Netball Drills – Age 12–16
2nd edition
Anna and Chris Sheryn

101 Youth Hockey Drills
2nd edition
Stuart Dempster and Dennis Hay

anna and chris sheryn

youth netball

101 drills

drills

age **7** to **11**

BLOOMSBURY

LONDON • NEW DELHI • NEW YORK • SYDNEY

Published in 2005 by A & C Black, an imprint of Bloomsbury Publishing Plc
50 Bedford Square
London WC1B 3DP
www.bloomsbury.com

Second edition 2010
Reprinted 2013

ISBN (print) 978 14081 9996 1
ISBN (ePDF) 978 14081 0824 6
ISBN (ePUB) 978 14081 7417 3

Acknowledgements
Cover photograph by Getty Images
Textual illustrations by Q2A Solutions and Mark Silver
All photographs courtesy of Getty Images

Note: While every effort has been made to ensure that the content of this book is
as technically accurate and as sound as possible, neither the authors nor the pub-
lishers can accept responsibility for any injury or loss sustained as a result of the
use of this material.

A & C Black uses paper produced with elemental chlorine-free pulp, harvested
from managed sustainable forests.

Typeset in 10/12pt DIN regular
Printed and bound by CPI Group (UK) Ltd, Croydon, CR0 4YY

10 9 8 7 6 5 4 3 2

CONTENTS

ACKNOWLEDGEMENTS

Thank you to my enthusiastic guinea-pigs at Ashgate Netball Squad and all the children at Cowling Primary School Netball Club. Also, thank you to all those coaches of netball training sessions I have enjoyed over the years, from school to county.

INTRODUCTION

Netball is a fantastic, competitive team sport played by over one million women and girls each week in the UK alone! Accessible to all ages and abilities, netball is a skilful, physical, athletic game that provides opportunities for both social, fun activity as well as competing at the highest levels.

The aim of this book is to give coaches, teachers and parents a resource to construct effective drill sessions to introduce young players to netball. It is important for all netballers to be able to consistently perform the simple things well, and learning good habits at the start will provide a good foundation for any young player. The drills included are designed to introduce the basic skills and concepts and include the common themes of movement and core passing and catching skills. Some drills therefore cover the same skill elements in a slightly different way, helping to add some variety to keep the sessions interesting – remember the key objective of any practice session is to ensure the players want to come back for the next one. Their experience in these early years can determine whether they continue to play (at any level) into adult life, and also has the potential to influence their view of sport in general; this can be seen as an enormous responsibility or a real opportunity! It can certainly provide some wonderful rewards.

All players, and in particular young players, need to have fun and enjoy their netball, which includes their training; it is important not to burden them with abstract concepts or complicated tactics that they will not understand or be able to perform and which can potentially erode their confidence. For this reason there is a strong sense of fun running through all the drills and the opportunity to introduce a little imagination – if they can learn and not notice they are doing so whilst enjoying themselves, you have succeeded.

KEY TO DIAGRAMS

GS	Goal Shooter
GA	Goal Attack
WA	Wing Attack
C	Centre
WD	Wing Defence
GD	Goal Defence
GK	Goal Keeper
△	cones
- - - - -▶	movement of ball
⎯⎯▶	movement of player

SESSION GUIDELINES

communication

In any sport, on most training nights you will see a coach working with young players struggling to form them into pre-drill formations. Instructions such as 'Get into a circle' or 'I need two staggered lines' often result in formations that owe more to a stage farce than a netball session. This leads to exasperated coaches, confused children and wasted time.

Never fear – here are some tips to help overcome some common problems:

Watch your language

I know an excellent tennis coach who, when working with a group of 6–8-year-olds, told them to 'Stand in the tramlines'. I mentioned to him afterwards that the reason that not all of them responded was that many of them had no idea what a tramline was, and even less idea which area of the court he was talking about.

Try at all times to take account of the age and experience of your players before you speak. Avoid jargon like the plague, explain what you mean and constantly question and re-evaluate your use of language. If you want to test yourself, ask a non-netballer to watch a session and keep a list of all the terms that they do not understand. Have a look at the list and then ask yourself what you really meant! For example, if you refer to the 'D', be aware that most seven- or eight-year-olds will know 'the letter D' as 'the duh sound', and in their world a 'D' is actually a 'd' and looks nothing like what you wish to convey.

'Get into pairs/groups of three etc.'

This instruction will rarely elicit a prompt response as junior politics will come into play ('where's my best friend' etc.) and few players will have the foresight to move around to find a partner.

With young players, the best way to deal with this is to designate two points (or markers) as 'Ones' and 'Twos'. Then simply touch each player on the head, look her in the eye (important!) and give her a number. As soon as a player has a number, she should go and stand at the relevant marker. (Top tip: make sure that the markers are well spaced – if they are too close, the groups will intermingle and when you look around you will find that you have only created another heaving mass of humanity elsewhere on the court.) Then the first player in the 'Ones' line pairs up with the first player in the 'Twos' line, and so on.

You can pair up older players by asking everyone to put their hands in the air and keep them there until they have a partner. In this way it is easier for everyone to see who remains.

'Make a circle'

Ask a group of players (of almost any age) to form a circle, and what you get will likely resemble a football crowd. A good way to achieve an evenly spaced circle is to ask all the players to hold hands and then slowly walk backwards as far as they can without letting go. You will be left with an evenly spaced circle.

'Form a staggered line'

In a number of the drills in this book you will need the players to form two parallel lines in a zigzag formation. This, again, can be a real struggle. The easy way to do this is in four steps:

1   Ask the players to form a single line and then hold hands.
2   Spread them out until they can only just hold onto each other – they will then be evenly spaced.
3   Number alternate players one and two – 'One, two, one, two' etc.
4   All number ones stand still. All number twos walk out to form the second line. When both lines turn to face each other, they will form the perfect 'zigzag'.

building drills

When you are introducing complex drills to groups of players, always explain each element separately so that everyone is clear about what they have to do before they start. By flooding the group with information, you run the risk of the drill becoming disorganised or falling apart. For example, if the drill involves a run–receive–land–pass sequence, demonstrate and describe the run and land only at first so that everyone can see and understand what a good job looks like. Only add the next element when the basics are spot on. There is absolutely no point in introducing a ball to a drill if the running and landing principle is not understood.

quality before quantity every time

Building an environment of excellence can be achieved without becoming boring. Just be very clear and concise about the skills you are about to practise and then concentrate on quality of execution at all times. Do not be drawn into lengthy drills that test stamina and reduce quality of play – short, sharp, top-quality drills will ensure that top-quality play is ingrained.

Remember: 'Practice does not make perfect; it makes permanent'. If sloppiness is part of the training regime, it will become ingrained in performances.

the learning curve

The development of a skill during a group practice will not follow a straight line. It is usual for awareness and concentration initially to be high, and for skills to develop at a corresponding rate. However, as the drill progresses concentration levels will fall and therefore so will players' accuracy. If this is allowed to continue unchecked by the coach, competency levels and enjoyment levels will suffer.

To address this issue, coaches must constantly be aware of the pattern of the players' concentration levels and take time to rest their minds and bodies. Stop the drill, re-communicate the objective and the skills involved and then, once the players are rested and ready – both mentally and physically – start again. If necessary, change the drill to something the players are familiar with and can do, then return to the original drill later. In this way the inevitable decline in competency can be arrested and the development curve can be edged upwards.

confidence

When boys encounter problems they are likely to blame the ball, the weather, the passer – anything but themselves. With girls, the first port of call tends to be their own performance. This means that the coach must ensure that confidence is not undermined by progressing drills too quickly for the ability of the players. Instead, provide drills that provide initial success, and progress slowly. Always focus on what has gone right and not on perceived failures.

warming up

A 'warm-up' is necessary to prepare the body for exercise, but children need less warm-up time than adults and contrary to traditional wisdom, there is no evidence that stretching *before* exercise improves performance or reduces the risks of injury. Instead, stretches should be performed *after* exercise.

Whilst children need less warming up, introducing this as part of a training session is a good habit to get them into. It is also a good way to get them engaged and focused on netball, rather than whatever they were doing before! It helps to get them ready for the rest of the session. For youngsters, it is important to make the warm-up fun and varied – keep it moving so they don't get bored. Don't strive for perfection – use a little imagination and they will join in with enthusiasm.

A warm-up should consist of similar movements to the exercises players are about to perform. There is no point running around the court for 10 minutes if you are then going to perform a series of sprints or jumps. Think about the range of movements that you are preparing the players for and gradually build up the intensity from gentle warm-up to near-performance level.

Be careful not to warm up for too long to avoid using up energy that should be reserved for playing. Players will need to sweat a little, but shouldn't be fatigued by the warm-up. A good rule of thumb is to elevate the heart rate to the extent that players are sweating lightly and are mildly out of breath.

warming down

This tends to be a much ignored area of coaching sessions and as mentioned above, the warm down is the place to work on flexibility. Children have a natural flexibility and whilst muscle fatigue and stiffness is not likely to be a major issue for the young player, awareness of warming down is again a good habit to get them into.

If stretches are carried out consistently during a warm down this can avoid muscle stiffness and soreness in the days following matches; more important for older players.

Structure the warm down to target any specific areas of the body that have been worked during the session, for example, if you have included lots of jumping drills make sure the warm down includes some stretches for the legs (such as calf and hamstring stretches).

drill categories

The drills in this book are divided into the following categories:

1   Warming up
2   Movement and footwork
3   Ball skills – passing and catching
4   Attacking and defending
5   Shooting
6   Game scenarios
7   Conditioned Games
8   Warming down

Some of the drills are basic and introduce skills and techniques for young and inexperienced players, others are more advanced and should only be selected for more confident and experienced players. You can select drills from across the sections to make up a varied and interesting session.

Whilst variety helps keep players and coaches interested, some of the basic skills take time to learn and there is no harm in revisiting drills, or having a set routine as part of the warm-up session. We all have favourites and as long as there is a mix of basic skill levels and activity-based drills within a session, everyone should have some fun whilst they are learning.

session structure

There are as many ways to compile a session as there are coaches. There are some basic guidelines that will help a session make sense for players and coaches. The length of time for a training session will vary depending on the age of the players – an hour session is a long time for very young players to concentrate and be physically active. A 45 minute session would be better. It is good to finish a session in a well-structured, controlled way rather than it fizzle out because players have lost interest or are too tired.

A key element to your session for this age group is to interest them enough to come back for the next session.

A golden rule: always ensure the session ends on a positive note, even if this is a game of ladders, ball thief or another favourite.

Typical session structure:

At the beginning let players know what you will be working on in the session. For young, inexperienced players it is good to pick one type of skill or new technique and concentrate on that throughout – don't confuse them with trying to introduce too many things at once. (This goes for all ages at times!)

As the sessions progress and your group becomes more confident, reminders of skills covered in previous sessions are good. Remember, build on skills slowly to improve confidence, encourage quality and instil good habits.

1 Warm-up (maximum 10 minutes)

The aim is to get them ready for the session and focused on you and netball. Include drills that introduce some basic movement techniques and aim to finish this section with a game-based activity from the warm-up drills to add a fun element.

2 Drills (maximum 20 minutes)

Select the drills depending on the objective for the session. In some cases the drills provide a natural progression and it will be clear which drills to use first. Only progress the drills if there are clear indications that the players are coping and developing good technique.

Some people will pick up the drills more easily than others; allow time to be able to explain the drill and what you want them to do, and to demonstrate the technique so they can see a good example first. Be prepared to let them try out the drill and then reset your expectations of what they need to do if necessary – remember: look for quality.

Be careful not to 'over drill' a technique – you don't want them to get bored or frustrated. There is no harm in coming back to a drill at a later stage if players are not achieving the quality you are looking for. It helps to have a couple of reserve drills up your sleeve to use at short notice if a drill is not working well – this is particularly useful when introducing some of the more complicated drills that require more concentration and co-ordination.

3 Play netball (minimum 10 minutes)

Players of all ages have one thing in common – they prefer playing to practising! Make sure they get the chance to play netball in every session, even if only for a short time.

This can be as part of a conditioned game to help introduce a skill or technique into a game situation, or as a game scenario to practise a specific move or sequence, such as a centre pass.

Keep players moving and changing in if you have extra numbers. Encourage observers to help watch out for good skills and give lots of praise for successes and players trying hard. It is a good idea to set targets for players within the game other than scoring goals – goal scoring can be seen as the most important thing for young players and they may feel left out if not playing in a shooting position. Set them targets of number of passes, interceptions, centre passes etc., whatever works for the group and you!

A sense of humour on court is essential, not only to help keep the coach sane, but it can also remove tension that can make players less inclined to try hard and risk making a mistake. Enjoy it and have fun!

4 Warm down (5 minutes)

Don't miss this bit out! Whilst young players have less need for stretching as their natural flexibility is better than adults, this gives you the chance to reaffirm the skill/objective of the session and finish on a high note.

improvising equipment

There are few groups that enjoy unlimited budgets, so here are some ideas for ways to improvise kit.

Ideally	Alternatives
Beanbags	Rolled-up football socks or socks filled with dried peas and sewn closed
Hoops	Chalk circles or lengths of rope tied into a loop
Cones	Margarine lids and some poster paint to provide colour designations when required
Skipping ropes	Lengths of washing line make excellent substitutes and in fact are far superior to rope, which turns far too slowly
Bibs	Old T-shirts with the necks and arms cut off, painted with cold-water dyes and spray-painted letters – this might not look good but is great fun for kids to make and saves lots of money

England's Sara Bayman marking Australia's Madison Browne trying to prevent an easy pass into the goal circle (World Series 2009).

WARMING UP

As previously mentioned, the warm-up is an important part of the session. While there is no evidence to prove that a warm-up aids performance or helps to avoid injuries, experience tells us that a relevant and focused warm-up prepares both mind and body for the practice. The warm-up is also an opportunity for the players to weigh up a new coach, so if you are new to the group make sure that your session is well planned, clear, well delivered and, above all, fun!

Contrary to traditional wisdom, the warm-up is not the place to improve flexibility (save this for the warm-down when the muscles are warm). The warm-up should be controlled and replicate the types of activities that you will be focusing on in the body of the session. So, three times around the court then touch your toes is not really what we are after!

The following drills provide some ideas for warming up with and without the ball, including some basic movement and mobility exercises and some game-based activities. Always follow the same rule – build speed and intensity gradually and focus on quality of movement. Finish the warm-up with a game-based activity and they should be raring to go!

drill 1 *around the court*

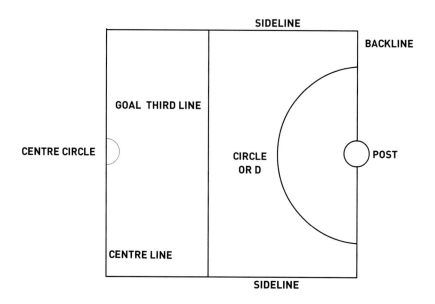

Objective: To warm up and ensure everyone is familiar with the different areas of the court. This drill is ideal for young netballers, and not so bad for experienced players either!

Equipment: Half the court.

Description: Spread the players around the area. The coach shouts out the name of one of the lines and points on half a court (e.g. 'sideline!') and all the players race to that point. The coach then shouts another position (e.g. 'D!') and the players race there.

Coaching points: When working with new or younger players, add different points slowly, starting by repeating two or three and only adding one at a time. In this way the positions will become ingrained. It can be made into a game for younger players with the last players to an area being 'out'. This can be played individually or in teams.

Progression: With older players, ask them to move around the half court and then call two or three points in quick succession. The players then have to make a quick decision on the fastest way to reach all points.

drill 2 *fast mice*

Objective: To warm up the body and develop foot speed.

Equipment: Half the court.

Description: The players start by standing on the sideline facing into court. They then have to reach the centre of the court using very fast feet and tiny steps. The objective is to complete as many tiny steps in the shortest amount of time. As with all these animal drills, you can make it as fun as possible by asking the players to imitate a mouse – noises and all.

Coaching points: Younger children will lose concentration and form very quickly and will increase the step length in order to move forwards quickly. Re-emphasise the objective of the drill before each re-start. The race is not to see who moves forwards fastest, but who can get the most steps in during the specified distance. Ensure that the forward motion is steady.

Progression: Try a timed race – who can perform the most steps in, for example, 10 seconds.

drill 3 *knees and heels*

Objective: To warm up and introduce dynamic stretches.

Equipment: Half a court.

Description: This can be performed in teams depending on numbers. Players line up along the sideline facing into the court area. They jog across the court lifting their knees high as they go. When they reach the other side they turn round and return doing heel flicks. Heel flicks should be done at a slow pace with players flicking their heels up to reach their bottom as they move.

Coaching points: For young players keep this drill short and reduce the space if necessary. The emphasis should be on controlled movements to help stretch out the quads and hamstrings while on the move. Movement should be balanced with players maintaining an upright position throughout each movement, using their arms to help with balance. This can be performed as a relay with a group of players on each sideline taking it in turns to complete high knees and heel flicks.

drill 4 *stomping giants*

Objective: To develop strength and improve movement abilities.

Equipment: Half the court.

Description: More foolishness! Starting on the sideline, ask the players to march out to the centre of the court pretending to be the biggest, loudest giant imaginable. Each stride must be as long as possible, each leg lift must be as high as possible and the drill must be performed under control. The objective is perfect form, not speed.

Coaching points: Encourage straight legs during this drill.

Progression: Give each 'giant' a marker (anything will do – margarine-tub lids are fine). Ask players to stomp out for eight strides, put down the marker and, after walking back to the start, try to reach their marker in fewer strides the next time.

drill 5 *creepy crabs*

Objective: To increase the body's range of movement.

Equipment: Half the court.

Description: The players start by standing on the sideline facing one end of the court. On the coach's signal, they start moving sideways into the centre of the court. The drill should be performed in both directions, left to right and right to left. Make it fun by asking the players to imitate a crab with nippy pincers (hands) and lots of crabby noises!

Coaching points: It is important that the path of movement is sideways and that the upper body doesn't creep around. To achieve this, the players should perform the drill while the coach remains on the sideline. The players must look at the coach as they perform the drill, which will stop them from twisting.

drill 6 *jumping crabs*

Objective: To increase the body's range of movement.

Equipment: Half the court.

Description: The players start by standing on the sideline facing one end of the court. On the coach's signal, they start jumping sideways into the centre of the court. The drill should be performed in both directions, left to right and right to left.

Coaching points: It is important that the path of movement is sideways and that the upper body doesn't creep around. To achieve this, the players should perform the drill while the coach remains on the sideline. The players must look at the coach as they perform the drill, which will stop them from twisting.

   The objective of this drill is to achieve height and 'hang-time', so encourage the use of arms to drive the body up and gain height.

drill 7 *froggies*

Objective: To warm up the body and develop explosive power for jumping and speed work.

Equipment: Half the court.

Description: The players start on the sideline, squatting with their hands flat on the floor and hands between their knees. On coach's command, each 'frog' must spring as high as possible and land again in the starting position. For fun, the players can compete for the loudest or best 'froggy' sound. Five springs forwards is plenty, then players walk back to the start. Repeat three times.

Coaching points: Concentrate on height and form at all times, ensuring that the players return to the start position before performing the next repetition. As they tire, they will be tempted to jump from a semi-squat position. This will not deliver the same benefit.

drill 8 *crazy groups*

Objective: To encourage concentration using a fun warm-up.

Equipment: Players.

Description: On the coach's command the players must form groups as per the instruction. For example, if the coach calls 'Fours!' the players must form groups of four, all holding hands with each other, and so on.

Coaching points: Once the players have grasped the principle of this drill it can be introduced unexpectedly (with a prize for the first group to form correctly – chocolate buttons work wonders!) into any part of the session, just to keep everyone on their toes.

Progression: Add four different coloured cones around the perimeter of the working area. On the coach's command all the players have to run around the designated cone before forming into their groups.

drill 9 *dodge tag*

Objective: To practise dodging skills and improve balanced movement.

Equipment: Players.

Description: The playing area selected should be sufficient to allow the players to run around but not so large that it allows full freedom of movement. One third of the court is ideal, or you can reduce the size of the area of movement using cones. Two players are taggers (T). The rest of the players must dodge out of their way and avoid being tagged. Players who have been tagged must stand still, creating barriers for the other players to dodge around.

Coaching points: Youngsters can get a bit excited and run into each other. Watch out for controlled movement and encourage players to avoid each other. One danger is players being hit by flailing arms, so warn the group first.

Progression: Reduce the size of the playing area and increase the number of players 'on'.

drill 10 *copycats*

Objective: To improve reactions and get players moving.

Equipment: One third of the court and one ball.

Description: The players space out in one third of the court and stand facing the coach, who stands in the centre circle with a ball. On command, all players start 'fast feet' on the spot and watch the ball. The coach moves the ball to different positions at random, for example high left, high right, in front and so on. All the players must react by stretching their arms in the same direction as the ball.

Coaching points: Look for players maintaining fast feet throughout – the movement should be balanced and controlled. Encourage quick reactions.

Progression: The coach throws the ball up, left or right, and players react by jumping in the relevant direction. The coach drops the ball, and players react by touching the floor (straight down, to the left, or to the right) and immediately jumping back up. The coach can also drop the ball behind her, at which point all players must sprint to the opposite goal third. (For young players, keep sprints to a minimum.)

drill 11 snakes

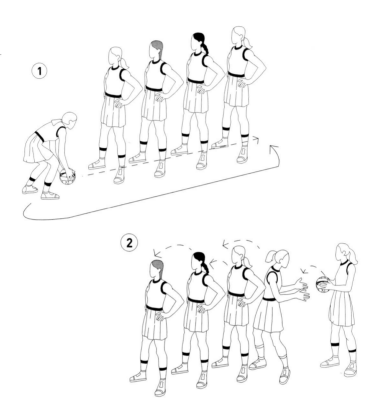

Objective: To warm up and have fun!

Equipment: One ball per team.

Description: Divide the group into teams, with a maximum of six players per team. Each team lines up with the players one behind the other, 1 m apart with legs apart. Player A is the first player in the line and has the ball. On the coach's command, A rolls the ball through the legs of the other players in her line, then races to take up position at the end of the line and catch her own roll. Facing forwards, she picks up the ball and passes it to the player in front, who takes the ball in both hands and twists the opposite way to give the ball to the next player. This left/right twisting motion is repeated until the ball is with the player at the front of the line, who starts the drill again by rolling the ball through the tunnel of legs once more. Repeat until all players have rolled.

Coaching points: While this is a 'young' drill, the twisting motion is a great warm-up for the upper body and with two teams racing each other it can be a lot of fun.

drill 12 name game

Objective: To warm up the body and have fun.

Equipment: Cones.

Description: Use the cones to set up a five-metre long grid. The players line up at the start line. The coach calls out a series of instructions; if an instruction applies to a player or players, they must run to the opposite side of the grid and back again. For example, 'All players with blonde hair; whose name begins with 'S'; who have a brother' and so on.

Coaching points: Look for short steps as the players accelerate, driving back with their elbows to pump the arms. The turn at the opposite side of the grid should be a sharp change of direction, not a slow curve. The players should drive away from this line too.

drill 13 duck duck goose

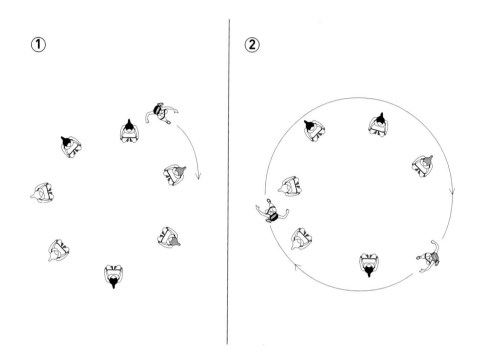

① ②

Objective: To develop balance when running, speed and quick reactions.

Equipment: Players.

Description: Choose one player to be the 'goose'; all other players are 'ducks'. The ducks sit in a circle facing inwards, with the goose on the outside of the circle. The goose walks around the circle behind the ducks, saying 'duck, duck, duck ...' as she passes each one. At random, the goose shouts 'goose' and taps the head of the duck she is standing behind. The aim is for the goose to run around the circle and take the space left by the duck before the duck catches her. The duck who is tapped on the head has to get up and chase the goose around the circle, aiming to tag the goose before she reaches the space in the circle.

Coaching points: Encourage runners to run close to the circle, using both arms and legs to help them run quickly and in control.

drill 14 ladders

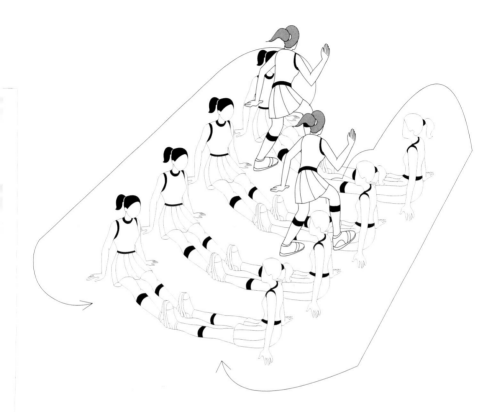

Objective: To develop balance while running, speed and quick reactions.

Equipment: Players.

Description: Pair players of similar ability and arrange as shown above, sitting facing each other with legs stretched out to make the rungs of a ladder. There should be a one-arm gap between the players in each team. Number the pairs 1, 2, 3 etc. The coach shouts a number and that pair have to jump up and race up and down the ladder. The drill is a race between the two teams to see who can get back to the starting place first.

Coaching points: It is important that the players keep their legs flat throughout the game to avoid tripping up the runners. The players also need to keep their hands close to their own bottom, or fingers will be stepped on.

Progression: More than one number can be called at once.

drill 15 *ball thief*

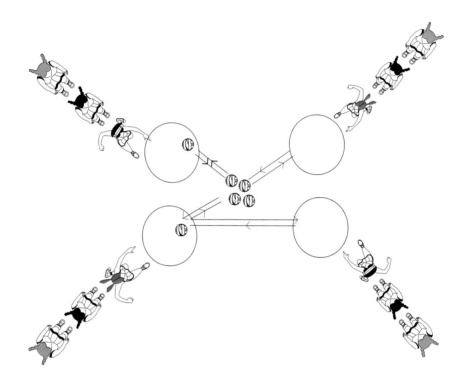

Objective: To warm up and develop good communication and speed.

Equipment: Four hoops and six balls.

Description: Place one hoop at each corner of a 5 m square. The hoops are 'home base' for each team. Divide the players into four teams and stand them in line, one team behind each base. Place six balls in the centre of the square. On the coach's command, one player from each team runs to the centre to grab one (and only one) ball, before returning to place the ball in their hoop. Then the next player in line runs to grab another ball. Once all the balls have gone from the centre the runners can steal a ball from the other bases. This continues until one team has three balls in their hoop. If no-one wins in a set time the coach can add another ball or two to make success a little easier.

Coaching points: Watch out for cheats picking up two balls at a time or stealing from bases before all the central balls have gone! Also watch for more than one player per team running at once. Encourage each team to talk to their runner so she knows what is going on around her.

drill 16 *the wall*

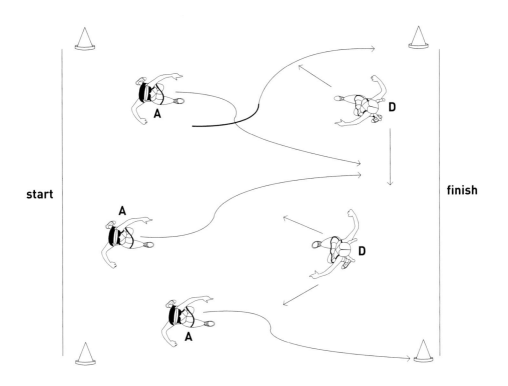

start

finish

Objective: To warm up by running, dodging and reacting to other players.

Equipment: Four cones.

Description: The size of the area used should reflect the age and number of players. Two or three defenders (D) stand in the middle of the playing area. On the coach's whistle the other players (attackers or A) try to cross 'the wall' of defenders to reach the other side of the playing area without being tagged. If a player is tagged she joins the defending wall.

Coaching points: Keep the grid small to encourage dodging and sprinting. Ensure players tag below shoulder height for safety.

Progression: Change the footwork patterns of the defending wall and running players. For example, they can run using side steps, and dodge using a push off one foot to change direction.

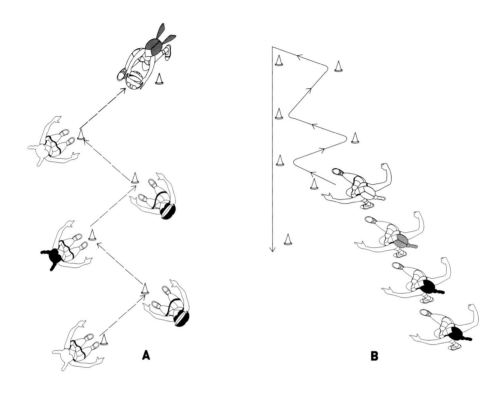

A   **B**

Objective: To warm up and practise passing skills. This drill may be unsuitable for younger players.

Equipment: One ball, cones.

Description: Divide the players into two teams. One team (A) spreads out in a zigzag formation about 3 m apart using half a court. This team passes the ball continuously up and down the zigzag. At the same time, the other team (B) runs in a zigzag over approximately two thirds of a court, running one at a time in relay fashion. The passing team counts the number of passes completed in the time it takes all the runners to complete the course. Any pass dropped is not to be added to the total. The teams then reverse roles and compare scores.

Coaching points: Look for accurate, balanced passing. For the runners, movement should be balanced and controlled using quick steps.

Progression: Vary the type of pass used. Vary the footwork pattern used.

drill 18 fireball

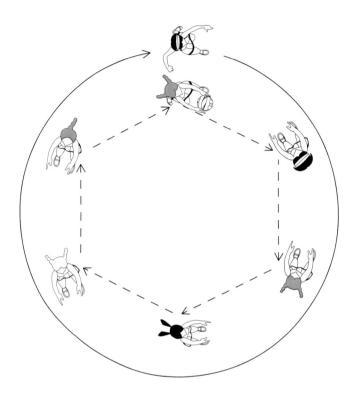

Objective: To develop passing confidence, quick reactions and balanced movement. Players need to be able to concentrate on the passing and be able to throw and catch, so this drill is not suitable for very young players.

Equipment: One ball.

Description: One player is the runner. The rest of the group stand in a circle. The aim is for the runner to sprint around the outside of the circle and return to her space before the ball is passed around the circle by the other players. The drill starts on the coach's whistle and continues with each player taking a turn as the runner.

Coaching points: Don't make the circle too big. Look for quick, accurate passing – the ball should be controlled, but should also leave the players' hands quickly, as if it were on fire! The runners should use quick, little steps to move around the circle – encourage them to keep their heads up and look where they are going.

Progression: The runner can move in the opposite direction to the ball. Introduce another runner and another ball – not for the faint hearted!

Larissa Willcox of the Mystics (NZ) getting free of her defender and jumping to catch the ball.

MOVEMENT AND FOOTWORK

Movement in netball is all about agility, change of speed and direction, and control; all of this requires body strength and balance. Good netballers are able to play at a fast pace, change direction, stop, and are always ready for the next pass and movement without falling over! Young players need to learn how to use their body strength to help with their stability and balance to control their movement and still be able to make a quick, accurate pass.

The footwork rule is a basic skill for young players to learn; once they are more confident with the idea of landing correctly, controlling their momentum and applying the footwork rule in the majority of situations, coaching can move on to focus on improving their balance, speed and control.

Landing is an important skill to master early; a balanced, controlled landing is the key to being able to make a quick pass, keeps the game moving and also helps to reduce the risk of injury. As players get more experienced, landing on one foot progresses to a running pass, where the ball is caught and released with the player still on the move, speeding up the game and leading to the fast-paced, athletic and attacking netball seen at higher levels.

Another key skill in netball is the art of dodging; a quick, decisive change of direction to outmanoeuvre or wrong-foot a defender and be free to receive a pass or create a space to move into. A dodge is often from a standing position and all players need to be able to master this skill whether an attacker or defender.

Introducing dodging to young players is a skill in itself for a coach! Young, inexperienced players do seem to run around a lot following the ball and lack the control of movement, change of pace or understanding of the game. Even more experienced players have been known to either stand still behind a defender and shout for the ball, or run backwards away from the thrower hoping they will lob the ball over the head of their defender. Encouraging a quick dodge and movement towards the thrower to make the pass easier takes time – don't give up and take this slowly as ability and experience will develop.

In this chapter, the basic landing techniques, footwork rule, pivot and dodge are broken down into simple component parts to help young, inexperienced players fully understand what is involved and practise good, basic technique from the start. Coaches can select the level of drill to use depending on the experience and ability of their players. The emphasis is still on having fun and the drills are designed to reinforce the skills needed in these key areas through repetition in different situations. The coach should focus on quality throughout.

key coaching points

Landing

1 Players should land with their body upright, feet about shoulder-width apart with feet and knees pointing in the same direction. If a player lands on one foot first, the other foot should be brought down quickly with the body weight evenly distributed to form the balanced support needed to make an accurate pass.

2 Players should land with their knees slightly bent; the landing should be cushioned by the ankle, knee and hip joints. Heads should be up looking at where they are going to make the next pass, with shoulders level and relaxed.

3 If players land with their knees over their toes their weight is too far forwards which makes it more difficult to control forward movement. The body weight should be more centred – this is sometimes more difficult for younger players to grasp and coaches need to be patient, encouraging upright landings to enable the players to learn this control.

Dodging

1 Weight should be evenly distributed with feet shoulder-width apart. Heads should be up looking towards the thrower.

2 The dodge involves a quick movement to one side and a quick transfer of weight and movement to the other side to catch the ball. The first movement should only be one or two quick side steps and then a stop.

3 Encourage players to control their movement and stop by grounding their outside foot and turning on the ball of their foot to move the opposite way, changing the weight to and turning their knees and hips to face the way they are moving.

4 Encourage this quick change of direction by coaching players to push off on their outside foot and transfer their weight to the other foot. This can be difficult for younger players to understand or control.

5 Encourage players to use their arms in a pumping action as they move to help control the movement and accelerate.

Pivoting

1 Encourage a controlled movement, holding the ball close to the body whilst looking up to see where they are going to pass the ball next.

2 The pivot, or rotation, should be away from the defender.

Golden rules

Balance and control are vital. Controlling the position of the body weight and posture will help players maintain their balance and this is the key aspect of good netball skills. Encouraging players to maintain a stable position with weight evenly distributed over both feet, heads and eyes up, and feet pointing in the direction they want to throw the ball – all are excellent habits to get into!

It is important for players to practise a balanced landing. Remember that halting a moving body requires a considerable amount of strength and coaches need to be aware this can be difficult for young players, particularly if they are excited and having fun! Keep the drills that involve lots of changes of direction nice and brief so the quality remains high and good habits are practised. There is no harm in rest!

Jumping to catch the ball can help young players to control their forward momentum and land without stepping. It doesn't matter if a player lands on one foot or two, the aim is to be balanced and ready to make the next pass. When on the move and catching the ball it is usual for a player to land on one foot then the other.

drill 19 cat and mouse

Objective: To develop spatial awareness and improve movement skills.

Equipment: One beanbag or football sock between two players.

Description: Divide the group into pairs. One is a mouse and the other a cat. The mouse tucks a 'tail' (the beanbag or sock) into the back of her waistband. The cat must see how quickly she can grab the tail. This drill is designed to help dodging skills so it is a good idea to remove the possibility of the mouse simply running off by restricting the space available, for example to one third of the court only.

Coaching points: Try to ensure that there is plenty of face-to-face dodging instead of just running and chasing.

Progression: To add some more fun have two cats and lots of mice in the playing area. If a mouse tail is grabbed, that mouse must replace her tail and wait, with legs wide, until a live mouse crawls through her legs to bring her back to life. Keep changing the cats and see how many tails they can catch in two minutes.

drill 20 *follow the leader*

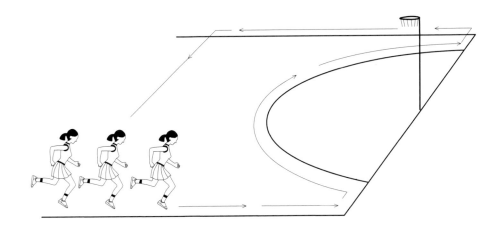

Objective: To practise the different footwork steps used in netball.

Equipment: The whole court.

Description: Select a leader (the coach may need to be leader to show the players the correct footwork patterns to use). Starting at one corner of the baseline, the other players follow the leader using the same steps and footwork patterns. Follow the directions as shown above, or let the leader choose the direction. The coach should choose from jogging, sprinting, side steps, and backward steps.

Coaching points: The aim is to keep the weight balanced, moving forwards with quick changes of direction pushing off from the outside foot.

Progression: For older players, introduce cross-over steps around the circle edge. This involves a sideways movement with one foot crossing over the front of the other. The weight should be slightly forwards on the front of the foot. Players need to use hips and shoulders to keep the movement balanced.

drill 21 *cats and dogs*

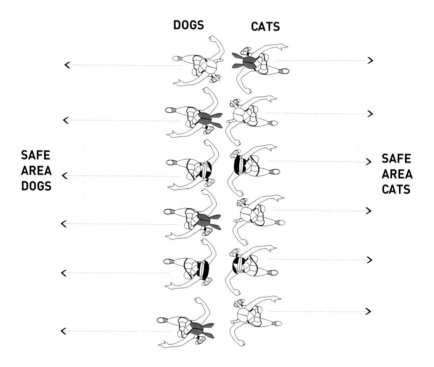

DOGS CATS

SAFE
AREA
DOGS

SAFE
AREA
CATS

Objective: To practise quick movement and improve reactions.

Equipment: Cones.

Description: Line the players up in two lines back to back. Start with either everyone standing or everyone sitting. One line is called the 'Cats' and the other line the 'Dogs'. If 'Cats' is called out by the coach, the players in that line have to run to a designated area, chased by their 'Dog' partner. If 'Dog' is called out, the 'Dogs' run and the 'Cats' chase.

Coaching points: Look for balanced movement, and quick responses.

Progression: Increase the working area to encourage more sprinting or decrease it to encourage more dodging.

drill 22 *jump*

Objective: To develop reactions, speed and introduce control of landing.

Equipment: Four different coloured cones.

Description: Set out the cones in a semi-circle approximately ½ m apart. The distance between the cones can be varied depending on the age and ability of the players. In pairs, player A stands approximately 1 m away from the cones in the centre of the semi-circle with the four cones in front of her. Player B stands facing her partner. Player B shouts a colour and player A jumps towards that cone and back to the centre as quickly as possible. When she returns to the centre, player B shouts another colour and so on. Swap roles after a short time.

Coaching points: The jumps and landings should be controlled. Encourage players to use their arms to help gain height and distance. When the player lands they should land on two feet and be balanced – no wobbles! Feet should be shoulder-width apart, head up and arms ready as if to receive a pass. Look for a cushioned landing with slightly bent knees. Players should be controlling their movement and be ready to make the second jump a quick reaction.

drill 23 *run and jump*

Objective: To practise balanced and controlled landing techniques.

Equipment: Play area approximately 1/3 court size depending on the number of players.

Description: The players jog around the playing area freely, on the coach's whistle they jump and land with two feet on the ground, arms ready as if to make a pass or catch a ball. Players stand still and wait for the instruction to restart.

Coaching points: Encourage players to move in all different directions. The jumps and landings should be controlled. Encourage players to use their arms to help gain height and distance. Players should land upright, on two feet and be balanced and stable – no wobbles! Feet should be shoulder-width apart, head up and arms ready as if to receive a pass. Look for a cushioned landing with slightly bent knees. Players should be controlling their forward movement. Give time for players to balance their weight before restarting the exercise.

Progression: As confidence grows increase the speed of movement around the area and reduce the time between restarting the exercise. Continue to encourage good technique though!

drill 24 run rabbit

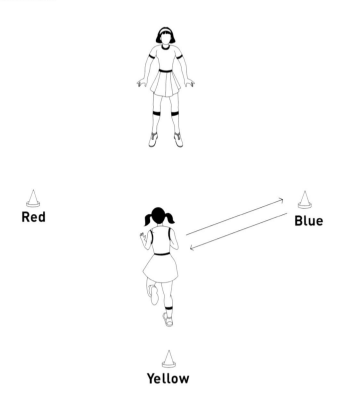

Red

Blue

Yellow

Objective: To improve reactions and practise different footwork patterns.

Equipment: Three different coloured cones between two players.

Description: Set out the cones in a triangle with approximately 2 m between each cone. Player 1 is working and starts in the centre of the triangle. Player 2 stands outside the triangle facing player 1. Player 1 starts fast feet movements on the spot. Player 2 will shout a colour to player 1, who must react by quickly moving to the correct coloured cone, touching it and returning to the centre of the triangle, facing player 2 at all times. When player 1 has returned to the centre, player 2 shouts out another colour. After a short time, swap roles.

Coaching points: Look for players maintaining fast feet throughout. The movement should be balanced and controlled. The working player should use side steps, quick steps backwards and so on to reach each cone. Encourage quick reactions and watch for players staying facing each other throughout.

Progression: Add another cone. Increase the working area.

drill 25 *change direction*

Objective: To practise quick, controlled changes of direction.

Equipment: Half the court.

Description: The players should space out within the working area. On the coach's whistle they jog in a straight line until they meet either a line or another player. When this happens they must change direction quickly by pushing off one foot and turning their body from the hips and shoulders, using their arms to help. Once they are facing in another direction, they carry on jogging until they meet another obstacle.

Coaching points: The change of direction should be a definite move, quick and controlled. The player is aiming to change direction without losing momentum and speed. It helps to exaggerate the arm and body movement, a bit like a child imitating a steam train!

Progression: Once players are comfortable with jogging, try increasing the pace. Cones placed at random in the working area can be added as extra obstacles.

drill 26 *footwork relays*

SIDESTEP, FAST FEET, SPRINT

Objective: To develop confidence in different footwork patterns and improve control and balance.

Equipment: Two cones.

Description: Divide the players into two teams. Set up the players in two lines as shown. On the coach's whistle, the first player from each team completes the course to the opposite line and tags her teammate, who continues back to her team mate on the opposite line. This continues until all players have completed the course. The coach should shout out different footwork patterns, such as 'jog', 'sprint', 'sidestep', 'backwards' and so on, and the players have to use these to complete the course.

Coaching points: Look for balanced and controlled footwork. Watch out for cheating!

drill 27 *the running line*

Objective: To introduce the difference between jogging and sprinting, and develop good sprinting technique.

Equipment: Three cones.

Description: Use the cones to mark out three 3 m sets. You will have the start line and then three further cones. The players line up along the start line and jog to the first cone, accelerate gently to the next cone and sprint at full pace to the final cone. Walk back to the start slowly to recover.

Coaching points: Look for a definite change of pace between the jog and the sprint. Encourage players to use their arms to help increase speed. Players need to be reasonably fresh, so allow plenty of rest between sets to ensure that every set is top quality.

drill 28 *the stepping rule*

Objective: To practise controlling forward momentum using a jump and to introduce the footwork (stepping) rule. To allow players to practise indentifying their landing foot.

Equipment: Court area.

Description: Line the players along a backline facing into the court area. On the coach's whistle players jog towards the next third line. Players should jump and land on one foot and then the other, aiming to land near the third line. Repeat down the court.

Coaching points: Start slowly and build up speed as confidence improves. Landing should be balanced and controlled with an even distribution of weight at the end of the movement. Players should not 'step' and should land with their body upright looking forwards, not at their feet! Young players often get confused over which foot they landed on first – ask players to identify their landing foot. This is the foot that must stay still to pivot in playing.

Progression: Increase the speed to practise control; this simulates sprinting in a game and is harder for younger players to do, so introduce carefully. Use alternate left and right foot landings.

drill 29 *footwork and ball*

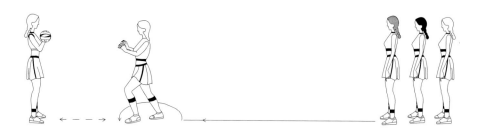

Objective: To introduce moving to catch the ball and practise making a balanced, controlled landing before making a pass.

Equipment: One ball, one cone.

Description: Select a feeder with the ball. A good quality feeding pass is important in this drill so to start it may be useful for the coach to be the feeder. Line the players up approximately 5 m from the feeder. Place the cone approximately 2 m from the feeder – this is a guide marker for the working player to jump forwards to land to catch the ball. The feeder must time the pass so the catcher can catch the ball as she lands. The catcher then returns the ball to the feeder and returns to the back of the queue. The drill is repeated for all players.

Coaching points: Start slowly and build up speed as confidence improves. Landing should be balanced and controlled. Players should land with their body upright, looking at the feeder to see the ball to catch it. Encourage players to have full control of their movement and an even distribution of their weight before making the return pass to the feeder. Encourage accurate passing.

Progression: Increase the distance and vary the type of pass used. More experienced players can time their jump and landing to receive a pass to their left and right as well as straight on. They would need to indicate (point) to the feeder where to make the pass as they make their run before they jump.

drill 30 snakes and ladders

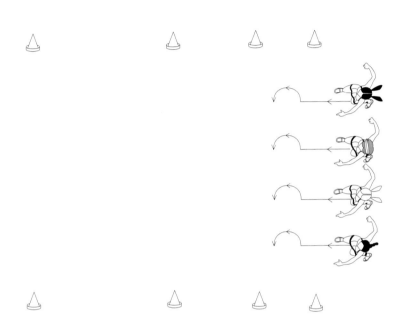

Objective: To reinforce good footwork.

Equipment: Eight cones.

Description: Use the cones to set up a ladder grid as above with the 'rungs' getting progressively further apart, starting at 1 m and ending at 5 m. All players stand on the start line. On the coach's command, they jog to the first cone, jump and land using good footwork. The players wait for the next command to jog to the second cone, and so on.

Coaching points: Allow a decent break (at least a couple of minutes) between runs to ensure that the players have the feeling of control before they start again. With young players, you can even turn this into a type of musical statues – they jump, land and freeze until the next command.

Progression: Once good practice is ingrained, speed up the run between cones. The faster the run, the more momentum there is to be controlled and therefore the harder the drill. If quality suffers, reduce the speed and build up again.

drill 31 *the pivot 1*

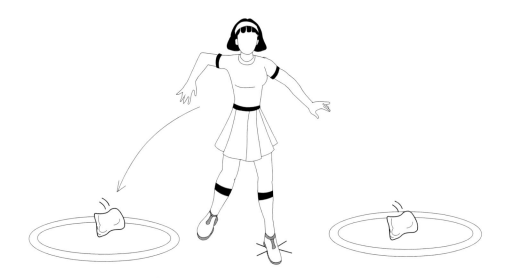

Objective: To introduce the pivoting movement to very young inexperienced players.

Equipment: Two hoops, five beanbags, chalk.

Description: Place the hoops about 1 m apart and chalk a cross on the ground exactly in between. Put the beanbags in the hoop on the left. The player starts by standing with her left foot on the cross. On the coach's command, she pivots towards the hoop with the beanbags in it, keeping her left foot on the cross at all times. She reaches down and picks up one beanbag, then pivots on her left foot again to drop the beanbag in the opposite hoop. Repeat until all the beanbags have been moved.

Coaching points: Encourage the players to get the feel of the pivoting movement on one foot. The stationary foot (which would be the landing foot in a game) must stay on the cross throughout the drill. The players need to be on their toes and should not drag the landing foot to move off the cross.

Progression: Once everyone has completed the drill pivoting on the left foot, repeat with the right foot on the cross and the beanbags being passed right to left.

drill 32 *the pivot 2*

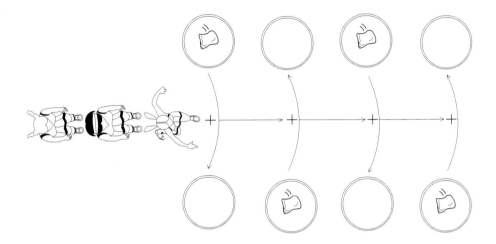

Objective: To progress the pivoting learning process.

Equipment: Eight hoops, four beanbags and chalk.

Description: Place the hoops in two lines of four approximately 1 m apart with a chalked cross in between each pair of hoops. Put one beanbag in diagonally opposite hoops, as shown above. The first player walks into the grid, places her right foot on the cross and pivots to pick up the beanbag on the right and then places the bag in the hoop on the left. The player then progresses up the grid pivoting alternately left and right to pick up and put down the bags in the hoop. On completion player 2 enters the grid and repeats the drill (obviously player 2 will start on the opposite side).

Coaching points: Encourage the players to get the feel of the pivoting movement and keep the landing foot still throughout the drill.

Progression: Set up two grids and two groups and race to see who can complete the drill first.

drill 33 *the pivot 3*

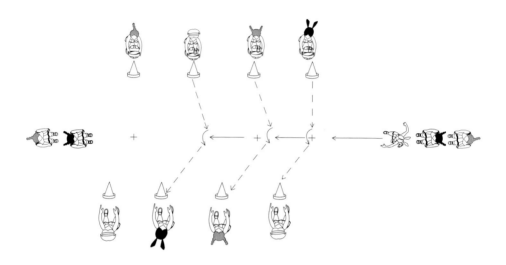

Objective: To progress the pivoting learning process. This drill may have to be reserved for more experienced players.

Equipment: Eight cones, one ball, chalk.

Description: Set the cones out in a staggered grid with a feeder on each cone and chalked crosses between each pair of cones (see diagram). The first player walks into the grid, places her right foot on the first cross and pivots to receive a pass from feeder 1 on her right, then pivots to make a pass to feeder 2 on her left. The player progresses up the grid, pivoting alternately left and right to give and receive passes. Player 2 then enters the grid and repeats the drill.

Coaching points: Encourage the players to get the feel of the pivoting movement and keep the landing foot still. Look for players facing the feeders to receive and pass the ball.

Progression: As players become more confident, increase the speed of the drill. Perform the drill as a relay race between two teams.

drill 34 *the dodge 1*

Objective: To introduce the basic techniques of dodging to young players.

Equipment: Two cones between two players.

Description: Place the cones approximately 3 m apart. Player A, the attacker, stands in between the cones with player B, the defender, standing in front facing the same way. In her own time, player A practises making quick, dodging movements to move away from player B staying within the area marked by the cones. Player B remains still. Swap roles to allow player B to practise the dodge move.

Coaching points: This is not a defender practice and is aimed at introducing the idea of quick, decisive movement with a change of direction. The defender is only there as a target to 'escape' from. Start slowly with two quick sidestep moves and build up the dodge movement as confidence improves. The attacker should start with a balanced stance, feet shoulder-width apart and knees slightly bent, looking forwards. Encourage a quick step to one side and a quick change to move in the opposite direction by pushing off on the outside foot – look for a turn on the ball of the foot and a transfer of weight with hips and shoulders facing the way the player is moving. Encourage players to use their arms in a pumping action to help with the movement.

Progression: When a quick change of direction with balance and control can be achieved with one step, encourage full movement away from the defender with arms out ready as if to catch the ball.

drill 35 *the dodge 2*

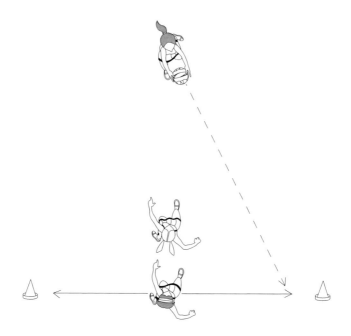

Objective: To practise dodging to get free from a defender and receive a pass.

Equipment: One ball and two cones between three players.

Description: Place the cones approximately 3 m apart. Player A, the attacker, stands in between the cones with player B, the defender, standing in front, both facing towards the feeder standing approximately 3 m away with the ball. On the coach's whistle, player A makes a quick, dodge movement to move away from player B staying within the area marked by the cones and receiving a chest pass from the feeder. Player B remains still. Swap roles to allow all players to practise the dodge move and feeding the pass.

Coaching points: This is not a defender practice and is aimed at introducing receiving a pass after a dodge. The defender is only there as a target to 'escape' from. The feeder must time the pass, which must be quick and accurate, to reach the attacker as she moves into the space away from the defender. Encourage good dodging technique with control and balance – see drill 34. To help the feeder know where to throw the ball the attacker should indicate (point) to where she will be moving before she makes the dodge.

Progression: Practise the dodge movement in both directions. Allow the defender to move and try and intercept the pass as confidence improves.

drill 36 racing snake

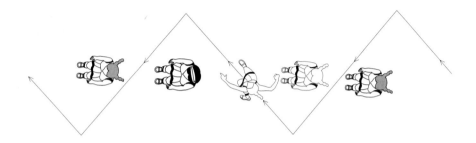

Objective: To improve speed and agility and practise dodging.

Equipment: Players.

Description: The players line up one behind the other all facing the same way, 2 m apart. On the coach's command, the player at the back of the queue runs up the line, weaving in and out of the standing players and facing the coach (who is standing at the head of the line) at all times. When the player reaches the front, she takes up position at the head of the queue and the next player runs.

Coaching points: Make sure that the runners are facing the front at all times, not following their nose in a looping path. In this way the players will be pushing off the outside foot to change direction. Encourage players to keep their heads up and look forwards rather than looking at their feet.

Progression: As the group improves, decrease the gap between players – the narrower the gap, the harder the player has to work. To introduce an element of competition, form two lines and have a race.

Renae Hallinan (Australia) looking to pass the ball demonstrating good, balanced shoulder pass technique.

BALL SKILLS – PASSING AND CATCHING

Good ball skills are obviously at the heart of netball, with the game depending on the players' ability to pass the ball with speed and accuracy down the court. The ability to vary their choice of pass to suit the situation and confidently pass the ball when under pressure from the opposing team's defence is key to success.

Good netballers need strong hands for catching and throwing. This is something most young players will lack, so ball skills will need to be developed gradually to improve confidence in throwing and catching and increase strength.

A common issue with younger, inexperienced players is that they consider possession of the ball to be the end in itself rather than a link in a team chain. This results in players following the ball around the court rather than moving into a space to receive it. Coaches need to encourage young players to be aware of the space on court as well as the ball – to think of more than just the next pass, but the next two or three passes.

As skills develop and drills require more movement, balance will become more and more important. Therefore, good practice is vital even within the more simple drills. Encourage a system of check–receive–pass–move, maintaining control and balance at all times.

When passing the ball, encourage players to:

- Keep fingers well spread behind the ball to help with control.
- Transfer their weight forwards from the back foot to the front to help give power to the pass.
- Look into the space where they are passing the ball and finish the pass by following the ball with their arm(s) and fingers extended in the direction they want the ball to go – this helps to avoid looping passes that take longer to travel the distance and are more easily intercepted.
- Pass the ball into the space in front of the receiver, ahead of their fingers, not behind them. The catcher might have to reach for the ball, especially if receiving a pass while on the move.

When catching a ball encourage players to:

- Watch the ball into their hands. Players often drop a ball because they are already looking to where the next pass is going to be.
- Stretch arms and fingers out towards the ball to catch it and step forwards to meet the ball rather than waiting for the ball to reach them. Fingers should be spread and 'W' shaped with thumbs behind the ball.
- Catch with two hands and snatch the ball into the body, cushioning the catch with bent elbows.

- Bring two hands onto the ball quickly if a catch is made with one hand to ensure control and balance for the next pass.

Younger players need to learn which type of pass to use when, the control and accuracy of the pass and understand the concept of throwing the ball into a space to enable the receiver to run onto and catch the ball more easily. This involves strength, balance, quick decision making and spatial awareness – difficult concepts to master!

Introduce different types of pass gradually, concentrating on the basic chest pass first to instil good throwing and catching techniques, with control and accuracy being key. A basic shoulder pass can be introduced as confidence grows – good technique here is vital to avoid the long looping passes that are easily intercepted and slow the movement of the game.

Young players have a tendency to throw looping lob-type passes which have little control or accuracy. A lob pass is a legitimate pass and requires good technique to be accurate. Don't accept a sloppy version as an alternative during practices – this will help reduce the chance of these passes being used in games.

coaching points

Remember the points above for passing and catching for all throws.

Chest pass: a pass aimed at covering short distances quickly. A good chest pass travels in a straight line from the thrower's chest height to the catcher's chest height – no loopiness!
Technique:

- Both hands behind the ball with fingers making a 'W' shape, with the ball held close to the chest and bent elbows relaxed at the sides.
- The fingers and wrists control and direct the pass.

Shoulder pass: a pass aimed at covering a greater distance and requiring a different technique to the chest pass. Thrown from shoulder height, the shoulder pass can be a one- or two-handed pass. This pass can be a direct pass travelling in a straight line from one player to another, or can be an angled pass looping over the head of a defender. When moving the ball up the court encourage players to make the shoulder pass a strong, straight pass and avoid the looped pass which is easier to intercept and is less accurate.
Technique:

- Stand side on to the person receiving the pass with feet shoulder-width apart, knees slightly bent and the body weight on the back foot. The opposite foot to the throwing arm is forward.
- The ball is held at shoulder height behind the shoulder with the elbow bent, either on one hand or with two hands.
- The ball is pushed forwards using the shoulder, elbow, wrist and fingers and involves a twisting movement from the shoulder and waist.

Bounce pass: a specialised pass aimed at covering a shorter distance and avoiding the arms of defenders. The ball takes longer to travel the distance because of the bounce, and accuracy is vital to avoid loss of possession through interceptions. A quick bounce pass into the circle to a shooter is a good way of avoiding good defence. This does require practice for younger players.

Technique:

- A bounce pass can be made with one or two hands from hip or waist height and from the side or the front of the body.
- The bounce should be approximately ²⁄₃ of the distance between the person making the pass and the receiver.

Lob pass: a specialised pass aimed at looping the ball high over the head of a defender. This can be used effectively to feed the ball into a shooter who is holding her space under the post. A lob pass can also be used throughout the court and should be selected because it benefits the team and not just as an excuse for a shoulder pass! Timing is crucial to avoid the defender intercepting from a well-timed jump and this also requires practice.

Technique:

- The pass can be made face on or sideways to the receiver.
- The ball is held in one or two hands above the head with elbows slightly bent.
- The ball is released from above the head using a push from the elbows and directed with the fingers and wrist.
- The ball travels in a high arc motion and the arms move upwards and forwards slightly as the ball leaves the hands, finishing high above the head.
- The highest point of the arc of the ball should be when it is over the defender's head, making it harder for her to intercept.

drill 37 *reaction drill*

Objective: To practise quick reactions and to develop hand–eye co-ordination.

Equipment: One ball between two players.

Description: Player A is working, with player B feeding the ball. Player A stands opposite player B, approximately 1 m apart. Player A lightly places her hands on her head. Player B drops the ball from different heights in front of player A, who tries to catch the ball before it hits the ground. The players take it in turns to catch the ball.

Coaching points: Quick reaction time is the key so players need to concentrate.

drill 38 *catch!*

Objective: To introduce basic catching techniques to ensure good habits and consistency. Aimed at young, inexperienced players.

Equipment: One ball between each pair.

Description: Players should stand facing each other approximately 2 m apart. Players pass the ball between each other aiming for good technique and no dropped balls!

Coaching points: This is a simple drill and should focus on catching. To catch the ball the catcher's partner has to pass the ball and good technique here should not be ignored – a simple chest pass should be used – see drill 43. Encourage the catcher to step forwards to catch the ball with arms and fingers extended to meet the ball as it moves towards them. They should watch the ball into their hands. Elbows should be bent as they catch the ball and it should be snatched in towards their chest. Their final position should be upright and balanced with a good, stable base – feet shoulder-width apart and shoulders level. Encourage this before they return the ball to their partner. See coaching points in the introduction to this chapter.

Objective: To improve reactions, increase ball awareness and develop passing.

Equipment: One ball.

Description: The players stand in a circle facing inwards. The coach stands in the middle with the ball and chest passes the ball at random to the players in the circle. The players must clap once before they catch the ball and then return the ball to the coach using a chest pass. Players must sit down if they drop the ball, don't clap before they catch the ball or clap to a faked pass.

Coaching points: Ensure quality at all times and do not allow wayward passes. When the players are more confident, they can be the feeders, but it is important that the feeders are able to throw consistent passes to keep the game moving. Players sitting out can join back in after a specified time, for example after three successful consecutive passes, or play until one player is left standing.

Progression: Use two feeders and two balls. Vary the type of pass, and add the rule that players must sit down if they use a different pass from the one in play.

drill 40 *wake up!*

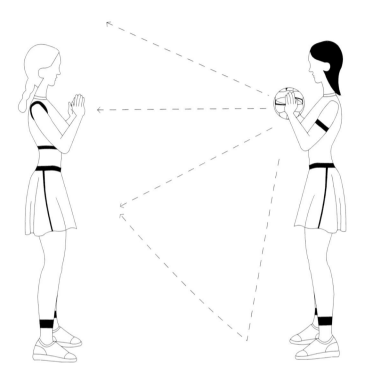

Objective: To encourage good reactions to the ball.

Equipment: One ball between two players.

Description: The two players face each other approximately 2 m apart. The attacker passes or drops the ball in any direction within arm's reach of the defender, who catches and returns the ball to the attacker using a chest pass.

Coaching points: All passes should be quick and are intended to catch the defender off guard. The defender should aim to stay balanced and in control of her movement and passes. Ensure quality at all times and do not allow wayward passes.

Progression: Forfeits can be included for wayward passes from either person, for example 10 star jumps. Introduce fast feet for the defender, when receiving the ball the defender should obey the footwork rule. Even with this fast feet movement the defender should work on the spot with little sideways movement.

drill 41 chest pass 1

Objective: To introduce the basic chest pass technique and develop confidence and co-ordination.

Equipment: A wall.

Description: The players stand a stride away from the wall and, keeping the feet still, lean forwards to put both hands flat on the wall with the fingers spread. On the coach's command, the players push away, trying to push themselves back to a standing position.

Coaching points: This is the first element for teaching a chest pass; it is not a strength exercise and should not be treated as such. This drill will give the player the feeling of the passing movement without the complication of having to direct a ball. This drill should be used sparingly as it is not very exciting, but it is a vital learning component when used in conjunction with the next three drills.

Objective: To develop confidence in good chest pass technique to ensure consistency and accuracy.

Equipment: One ball per player and a wall.

Description: The players stand 2 m from the wall and perform a chest pass against the wall, catching the ball on the rebound.

Coaching points: To help younger players, chalk a cross at chest height on the wall as a target for the pass. Encourage players to reach out to catch the ball rather than waiting for the ball to come to them.

Progression: As confidence and competence grow, try moving the players further from the wall and introduce races, for example to see who is the first to five consecutive successful passes.

drill 43 *chest pass 3*

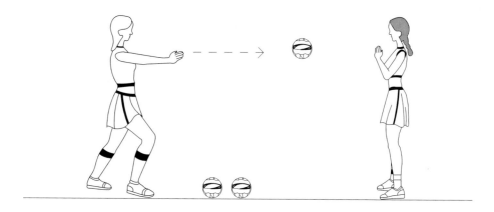

Objective: To develop confidence in good chest pass technique to ensure consistency and accuracy.

Equipment: One ball between two players.

Description: Players should stand facing each other approximately 2 m apart. Players pass the ball between each other using a chest pass aiming for good technique and no dropped balls!

Coaching points: Encourage a flat, direct pass from the chest height of the thrower to the chest height of the receiver – the ball should move in a straight line quickly. The thrower should use both hands, with fingers spread behind the ball. The ball is pushed with the fingertips pointing to the receiver and the player stepping from the back foot to the front to transfer her weight forwards as the ball leaves her hands. The step brings the hips, legs and body weight into the pass and adds power and speed. Remember good catching technique for the receiver – see drill 38 – catch!

drill 44 chest pass 4

Objective: To practise the chest pass.

Equipment: One ball per team.

Description: Divide the players into teams of eight. Set the teams up in a zigzag formation with approximately 2 m between teams. On the coach's command, the ball is passed up the line using a chest pass.

Coaching points: Younger players will get excited as they become engrossed in the game and will want to unload the ball quickly instead of executing a good pass. If this becomes a problem, tell the players that they are responsible for the ball until the receiver has caught it, so if a pass is dropped or missed then the passer has to retrieve it and run back to make a new pass.

Progression: This drill can be made continuous by asking the players to run to the end of the line after they have passed. If you have two teams, an element of competition can be introduced by setting a distance to be covered and seeing which team can do so the quickest.

drill 45 *shoulder pass 1*

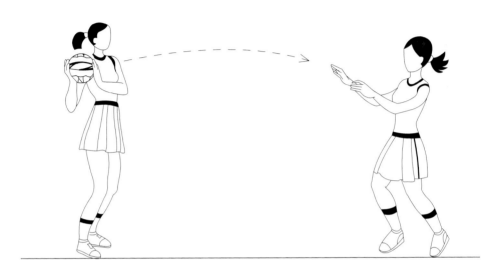

Objective: To develop confidence in good shoulder pass technique to ensure consistency and accuracy.

Equipment: One ball between two players.

Description: Players stand approximately 5 m apart. Player 1 has the ball, and player 2 stands with her hands up ready to receive the pass.

Coaching points: Focus on setting good habits with setting up the pass correctly and transferring the body weight in the direction of the pass to add power and distance. Encourage players to practise a one-handed shoulder pass with their dominant hand and a two-handed shoulder pass. Players should step forwards as they make the pass transferring their weight and twisting their shoulder to follow the ball – the end of the pass should result in their arm and fingers pointing in the direction of the pass, with their head up looking towards the receiver. Looping shoulder passes result from mistiming the release of the ball, or the arm movement pointing skywards instead of straight out at shoulder height. Shoulder passes that do not cover the distance lack strength and practising moving the body weight forwards in time with releasing the ball will add power. Keep everything slow and controlled to allow players to get the feel of the pass.

drill 46 *shoulder pass 2*

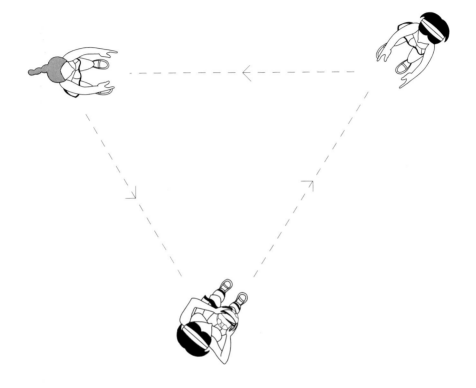

Objective: To develop confidence in good shoulder pass technique to ensure consistency and accuracy.

Equipment: One ball between three players.

Description: Set up the groups in a triangle with approximately 7 m between the players. On the coach's command, the ball is passed anti-clockwise around the triangle using a shoulder pass. Change the direction of passing.

Coaching points: The passing player is responsible for the ball until the receiver has caught it, so if a pass is dropped or missed then the passer has to retrieve it and run back to make a new pass. This will ensure accuracy rather than a quick off-load of the ball. Encourage good technique as described in drill 45.

drill 47 *shoulder pass 3*

Objective: To practise the shoulder pass.

Equipment: One ball per team.

Description: Divide the players into teams of eight. Set up the teams in a zigzag formation with approximately 7 m between teams. On the coach's command, the ball is passed up the line using a shoulder pass.

Coaching points: Younger players will get excited as they become engrossed in the drill and will want to unload the ball quickly instead of executing a good pass. If this becomes a problem, tell the players that they are responsible for the ball until the receiver has caught it, so if a pass is dropped or missed then the passer has to retrieve it and run back to make a new pass.

Progression: This drill can be made continuous by asking the players to run to the end of the line after they have passed. If you have two teams, an element of competition can be introduced by setting a distance to be covered and seeing which team manages to do so first.

drill 48 *the lob 1*

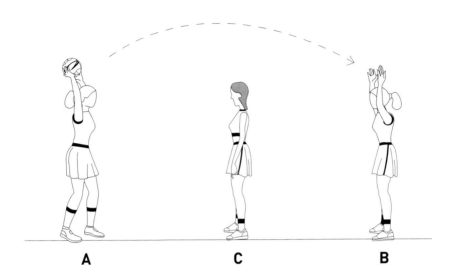

A   **C**   **B**

Objective: To develop confidence in good lob pass technique to ensure consistency and accuracy.

Equipment: One ball between groups of three.

Description: Player A stands with the ball facing player B, approximately 3 m apart. Player C is a defender and stands in front of player B facing player A. At this stage the defender should stand still to present a barrier between the thrower and receiver. Player A lobs the ball to player B aiming for good technique and over the head of player C. After five attempts swap roles.

Coaching points: Look for a controlled pass that loops over the head of the defender with the highest point of the arc of the ball being when the ball is directly over the head of the defender. Encourage the receiver to be ready to catch the ball with arms raised. Remember, young players tend to default to a lob type pass when under pressure – don't accept sloppy technique and instil good habits. This is an effective pass that can be used to feed a ball over a defender – it can also be easy to read and intercept for a determined, athletic defender!

Progression: As confidence and accuracy improves, encourage the receiver to jump to catch the ball in the air.

drill 49 *the lob 2*

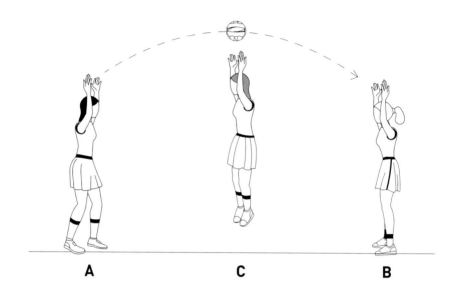

A   **C**   **B**

Objective: To continue to develop confidence in good lob pass technique to ensure consistency and accuracy.

Equipment: One ball between groups of three.

Description: This is a progression from drill 48, introducing an active defender which requires more accuracy from the thrower. Player A stands with the ball facing player B, approximately 3 m apart. Player C is a defender and stands in front of player B facing player A and should try to intercept the pass by jumping to catch the ball. Player A lobs the ball to player B aiming for good technique and over the head of player C. After five attempts swap roles.

Coaching points: Look for a controlled pass that loops over the head of the defender with the highest point of the arc of the ball being when the ball is directly over the head of the defender. Encourage the receiver and the defender to be ready to catch/intercept the ball with arms raised, and jump to try and snatch the ball out of the air. Watch out for contact from either player as they jump to catch the ball.

Progression: Introduce a second defender to try and mark player A as they throw the lob, facing player A with arms up. Watch for the correct distance from the new defender.

the toss-up

Objective: To introduce and practise the toss-up and improve reaction time.

Equipment: One ball between groups of three.

Description: The toss-up is a means of giving both players an even chance of catching the ball if an infringement on court is judged to be simultaneous by the umpire. Players A and B stand facing each other 1 m apart with their feet shoulder-width apart and hands by their sides. (In a game the players would face the way their team is shooting and all other players would need to be at least 1m away). The player with the ball (C) stands in between the players, close enough to be able to step forwards and hold the ball in the middle of A and B at shoulder height. Player C balances the ball on one hand with the palm facing upwards. She steps forwards to place the ball in between players A and B tossing the ball straight up to about shoulder height of the smallest player and at the same time shouting go. Players A and B both try to snatch the ball. If either player moves before player C shouts 'go' (or the umpire blows the whistle) the ball is given to the other player. The player who cleanly catches the ball gets one point. No points are given if the ball is dropped. After five attempts swap roles. As it is usually the umpire who takes a toss-up it is useful for players to be able to practise this with the coach responding to a whistle.

Coaching points: Look for a balanced position at the start. Players should be ready to move, knees slightly bent, with arms by their sides. Encourage players to watch the ball as the umpire/teammate brings it forwards to make the toss-up – this helps with anticipation and quick reaction. Encourage the players to snatch the ball into their body away from their opposing player.

drill 51 bounce pass 1

Objective: To introduce and develop confidence in the techniques of the bounce pass.

Equipment: One ball per player and a wall.

Description: Each player stands approximately 1 m from the wall and performs a bounce pass against the wall, catching the rebound. The ball should be 'pushed' towards the wall with the fingers pointing downwards. If a wall area is not available, work this drill in pairs.

Coaching points: To help younger players, chalk a cross approximately 30 cm from the wall as a target for the bounce. Ideally, players should not move their feet. In this way, accurate passing will be encouraged. If performing this drill in pairs, encourage players to make the pass reach their partner without the catcher having to move backwards. The bounce should reach about tummy height to make it easy to catch. Remember, this is an introduction to a specialised pass that should only be used in particular circumstances in a game, for example to feed the ball into the circle under the arms of a defender. It should only be used over short distances.

Progression: As confidence and competence grow try moving the players further from the wall and introduce races, such as the first to five consecutive successful passes.

Objective: To practise the bounce pass.

Equipment: One ball per team.

Description: Divide the group into teams of eight. Set up the teams in a zigzag formation, with approximately 2 m between teams. On the coach's command, the ball is passed up the line using a bounce pass.

Coaching points: Younger players will get excited as they become engrossed in the drill and will want to unload the ball quickly instead of executing a good pass. If this becomes a problem, tell the players that they are responsible for the ball until the receiver has caught it, so if a pass is dropped or missed then the passer has to retrieve it and run back to make a new pass.

Progression: This drill can be made continuous by asking the players to run to the end of the line after they have passed. If you have two teams, an element of competition can be introduced by setting a distance to be covered by the team.

drill 53 *turn and catch*

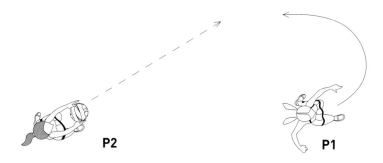

P2

P1

Objective: To develop quick reactions and catching skills and introduce the idea of turning the body to receive a pass.

Equipment: One ball between two players.

Description: Set up the players approximately 2m apart. Player 2 starts with the ball. Player 1 is working and stands with her back to player 2. Player 2 shouts 'left' or 'right' and player 1 must turn quickly in that direction to receive a pass. Player 2 should only pass the ball once player 1 has turned and is facing her. After five goes, swap roles.

Coaching points: Look for a quick reaction and a controlled turn by player 1. Passes should be accurate and timed to only be released when the player is ready.

Progression: Vary the type of pass. Increase the distance between players. When players are turning and receiving the ball confidently, the feeder can pass the ball into the space for the other player to move onto.

drill 54 *accurate passing*

Objective: To practise accurate passing with different passes.

Equipment: One ball between groups of four or more players, different coloured bibs or bands.

Description: Player A is the worker, the others are receivers. Line the receivers up facing player A with sufficient space between them to catch the ball without bumping into each other. Each receiver wears a different coloured bib or band. The coach shouts out a colour and player A must pass the ball to the receiver wearing that colour. The receiver returns the ball to player A. Allow all players the chance to practise making the pass.

Coaching points: This drill can be used for chest, shoulder and bounce pass. Work on each pass individually. Vary the distance between player A and the receivers depending on the type of pass being used. Focus on accurate passing with good technique.

Progression: Introduce a competitive element by getting groups to work in teams with points lost for dropped balls or inaccurate passing.

drill 55 *the box*

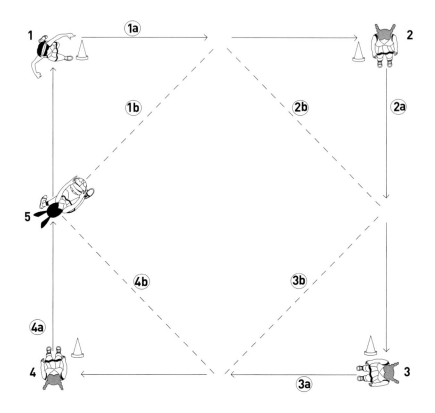

Objective: To practise passing on the move. This drill requires concentration and co-ordination so is only suitable for older, more experienced players.

Equipment: One ball and four cones per group.

Description: Divide the players into groups of five. Use the cones to mark out a square with approximately 7 m sides. Players each stand at a cone. Player 5 stands halfway between cones 4 and 1 with the ball. Player 1 runs towards cone 2 and player 5 passes ahead of her so that the pass will be received at the mid-point between the two cones. Player 5 then runs to the space left at cone 1. As soon as player 1 receives the ball, player 2 runs towards cone 3, player 1 passes to her, then runs on to cone 2 and so on.

Coaching points: This is a complicated drill so walk through the sequence first, then build up the pace. Look for a controlled, balanced landing. Each pass should be accurate and into the space the runner is moving into.

Progression: Vary the type of pass used.

drill 56 *throwers and catchers*

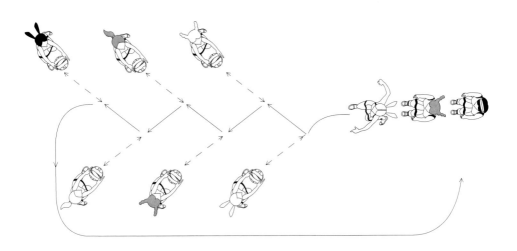

Objective: To improve passing and throwing confidence. Players need to be able to apply the stepping rule confidently.

Equipment: One ball between two players.

Description: Set up the players with the throwers in a zigzag approximately 5 m apart. The throwers start with a ball each. The remaining players are the workers and form a line at the end of the court. Player 1 starts sprinting towards the first thrower to receive a pass. Thrower 1 passes the ball ahead of player 1, who catches it and returns it to the thrower. Player 1 then pushes off quickly and changes direction to head straight to the next thrower, who passes the ball as above. This is continued until all the throwers have passed.

Coaching points: Look for the players sprinting hard into the space to receive the ball and a controlled, balanced landing. Each pass should be accurate and into the space the runner is moving into. Look for an accurate, balanced return pass.

Progression: Vary the type of pass used.

drill 57 *catching on the run*

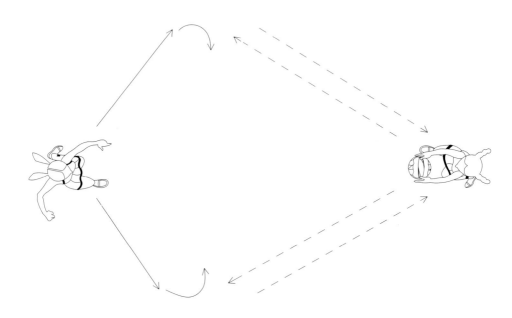

Objective: To practise throwing the ball ahead of a running player and catching a ball when on the run. This is a more advanced ball skills drill and is only suitable for older players.

Equipment: One ball between two players.

Description: In pairs, players stand approximately 2 m apart. Player 2 is the thrower and starts with the ball. Player 1 runs to the side and player 2 throws the ball ahead of player 1, who catches the ball, pivots and throws the ball back to player 2. Player 1 returns to face player 2, then runs to the other side and the steps are repeated. After five passes to each side, swap over roles.

Coaching points: Look for passes ahead of the running player to ensure they run onto the ball and don't have to reach backwards or stop to catch the pass. The landing should be balanced and controlled and the pivoting foot should remain still.

Progression: Vary the pass, introducing high or lob passes for example.

drill 58 *passing chain*

Objective: To develop passing confidence and teamwork.

Equipment: One ball and one set of bibs.

Description: Divide the players into two teams. Use one third of the court as the working area. Team A is the attacking team and starts with the ball. Team B is defending and aims to gain possession by intercepting passes. Once team B gains possession, the roles reverse. Possession also changes if the ball is dropped, the players break the footwork rule or the players go out of the working area. Each team gets a point if they link together a set number of consecutive passes or intercept the ball.

Coaching points: Look for and encourage short, sharp movements when getting free from defending players. Encourage players to run towards the ball to receive a pass rather than running away from it.

Progression: When players are more confident at using the whole space, restrict the pass so that a player cannot pass back to the player she received the ball from.

drill 59 *all change!*

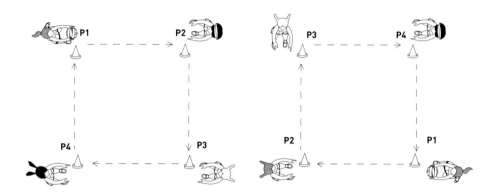

Objective: To develop confidence and improve accuracy and speed of passing.

Equipment: Four cones and one ball between four players.

Description: Set out the cones in a square with 2 m sides. The players stand in position, one at each cone. Player 1 starts with the ball. On the coach's whistle, the players pass the ball in turn, player 1 to player 2 to player 3 and so on, using a chest pass. Whenever the coach blows the whistle, the ball should change direction. If the coach shouts 'all change', all players must swap places and move to a different corner of the square. Once the players are back in position at a different corner, the ball begins to be passed around the players again. The first group to pass the ball around their square 20 times without dropping it is the winner.

Coaching points: Look for accurate passing with the players being balanced before making the pass, with their feet and fingers pointing in the direction they are passing.

Progression: Increase the size of the square and vary the type of pass used.

ATTACKING AND DEFENDING

Although there are defending (GK, GD, WD) and attacking positions (GS, GA, WA, C) on a netball team, all with definite roles, all players need to be able to adopt both an attacking and a defensive role within a game, depending on the situation. With younger players, the change between the two is often hard as it relies on the players understanding the flow of the game and being able to 'read' the play to anticipate what will happen next. These are advanced skills and will develop with experience and confidence.

The aim of this next section is to develop awareness of the attacking and defending roles and responsibilities, and when players should adopt a particular role. Getting a young player to recognise that their team has lost possession and they must now defend, that is mark their partner to try to stop them getting free to receive a pass or mark the ball with their hands high, is a huge achievement.

In addition, this section aims to develop controlled aggression, the desire to 'win' the ball, and the determination to gain possession and never give up – qualities that all good netballers possess.

key coaching points

1 Defenders need to have controlled, balanced footwork to be able to move quickly in all directions. They also need to be able to jump! It is surprising how many players seem to have their feet rooted to the ground, so encourage young players to jump and meet the ball whatever their size.
2 Defenders need to keep going and remain calm under pressure even when it appears that their efforts are wasted. This is hard for young players who can panic in pressure situations. Perseverance is a key quality for defenders. Try to ensure players understand how their efforts are having a positive impact on the game by putting off the attack or forcing mistakes, and encourage them to keep going.
3 The ultimate aim of the attackers is to score goals! Developing confidence in young players will help them work together as a team and improve their awareness of the space, each other and the passes they can use.
4 When attacking, i.e. in possession of the ball, encourage players to move towards the person with the ball and not run away or stand still! Moving towards the ball helps make the next pass easier. Players obviously have to work with the space and know to make a second or third move into a space for a pass, if the first attempt is not successful. Watch out for young, inexperienced players all running around the player with the ball like bees to a honey pot; encourage more thoughtful movement and space awareness around the court and remember: this is a hard concept for some young players and takes time to sink in!

golden rule

All players should be determined to get the ball and never give up chasing – it is surprising how many loose balls on court are reached or how many balls are prevented from going out of court by the dogged, enthusiastic player who chases every ball and never gives up!

As my netball teacher used to say, 'The netball court is the only place I want to see you snatching the ball!' A good habit to get into.

Sara Bayman of England is blocked from passing the ball by Australia's Natalie von Bertouch.

drill 60 *deception*

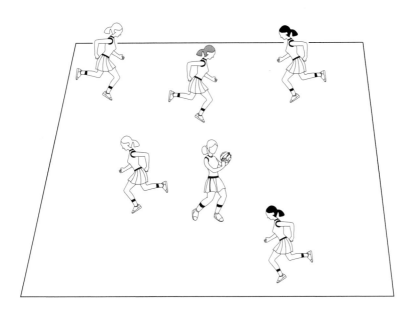

Objective: To practise faking a pass to confuse a defender, and to encourage players to watch the ball and expect a pass even if they are not being looked at.

Equipment: Players, one third of the court.

Description: Players jog around the playing area. On the coach's whistle, they get into the correct position to make a pass – feet shoulder width apart, knees bent and head up. A feeder stands in the middle of the group with the ball. At the coach's whistle, the feeder must have two players in her vision without looking directly at anyone, and should pass the ball to one of these players. If the feeder makes eye contact with anyone they are 'out'. Whoever receives the ball becomes the feeder.

Coaching points: Use two balls with two passers if the group is large. It is best to give each player two or three lives as young players like to be 'in' and playing. Players need to keep their heads up to be able to use their peripheral vision.

Progression: Include a defender to mark the receiver of the ball, who must get two other players in her vision and pass the ball to one of them.

drill 61 *scramble*

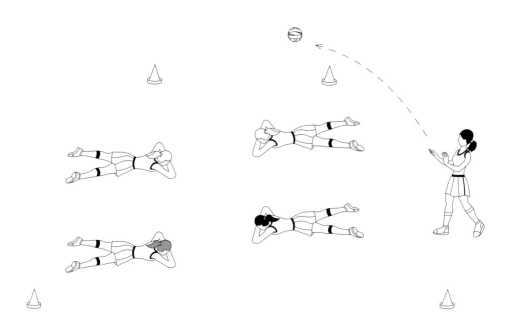

Objective: To encourage quick reactions to a loose ball – important for all players!

Equipment: One ball and four cones per group.

Description: Divide the players into groups of five. Mark out a square with 5 m sides using the cones. One player in each group is the feeder and the others are the scramblers. The scramblers start by lying down on their stomachs in the square with their eyes closed. (If it is too wet or cold to lie down, players may crouch down low with their eyes closed.) The feeder throws the ball in the air and shouts 'scramble'. The scramblers must jump up and scramble for the ball. The player who retrieves the ball throws the ball for the next scramble.

Coaching points: There needs to be space between the groups to avoid collisions and confusion. Encourage players to snatch the ball in to their chest to gain possession. Players must try to avoid barging each other out of the way.

Progression: Increase the size of the working area and combine two groups. Use two balls.

drill 62 *my ball!*

Objective: To practise competing for the ball in the air.

Equipment: One ball between three players.

Description: Divide the players into groups of three. The two working players stand side by side with their shoulders just touching. The feeder stands with the ball 2 m away, facing the players. The feeder throws the ball to the players, alternating between high and low passes. The players compete to see who can retrieve it first.

Coaching points: This drill can get quite competitive with some players, so encourage them not to barge each other out of the way! Look for players being 'ready' – up on their toes and watching the ball.

drill 63 *tipping*

Start ⟶

Objective: To practise jumping to tip the ball in the air.

Equipment: One ball between two players.

Description: Divide the players into pairs. Player 1 is working. Player 2 stands balancing the ball high above her head in one hand. Player 1 takes a short run-up and jumps high, aiming to tip the ball off the hand of her partner. She should aim to tip the ball and not knock the arm or hand of the other player, which would be contact in a game situation. If the ball is tipped, player 1 should try to catch it, or retrieve it quickly. Swap roles after five attempts.

Coaching points: It is useful to pair players of similar heights to make this drill even. Look for a controlled run-up and a correctly timed jump to tip the ball only. Encourage player 1 to chase the tipped ball and catch it if possible.

Progression: If the ball is tipped, both players should try to retrieve the ball – watch out for contact!

drill 64 *marking a player*

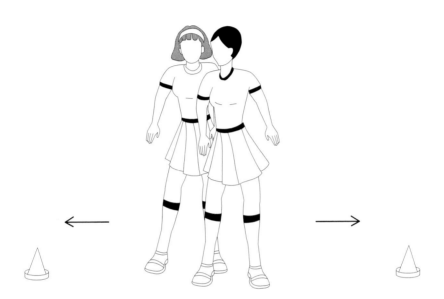

Objective: To introduce one-on-one defensive marking techniques.

Equipment: Two cones between two players.

Description: Place the cones approximately 3 m apart. The attacker stands in the middle of the cones with the defender standing in front, facing the same way. The defender's shoulders should be at a slight angle, but remain straight on to enable her to look over her shoulder at the attacker as well as at the ball. The attacker makes sideways dodge movements between the cones, changing direction at random. The defender aims to stick closely to the attacker, copying her movements.

Coaching points: One-on-one marking is where the defender stays close to the attacker, to restrict her movement and to intercept the pass. The defender should mark her partner without contacting her. The attacker should be holding a balanced 'ready' stance with her weight evenly distributed and on the balls of her feet with her knees slightly bent. When making the dodge movement look for good technique – see drills 34 and 35, although the focus for this drill is the defender. Encourage the defender to keep her shoulders only slightly angled towards the attacker and to use her peripheral vision; too much of an angle in her shoulders will over-commit her body weight to moving in one direction only and restrict her vision of the ball.

drill 65 *one-on-one*

Objective: To practise and improve confidence in the techniques for one-on-one defensive marking of a player.

Equipment: One ball and two cones between three players.

Description: Place the cones approximately 3 m apart. The attacker stands in the middle of the cones with the defender in front, facing the same way. The defender's shoulders should be at a slight angle, but remain straight on to enable her to look over her shoulder at the attacker as well as at the ball. The thrower stands opposite the attacker approximately 3 m away. The attacker must dodge to get free and receive a pass from the thrower. The defender aims to stick closely to the attacker and intercept the pass.

Coaching points: The attacker should be holding a balanced 'ready' stance with her weight evenly distributed and on the balls of her feet with her knees slightly bent. When making the dodge movement look for good technique – see drills 34 and 35, although the focus for this drill is the defender. Encourage the attacker to indicate (point) to where she wants to receive the ball. The defender should keep her head up, glancing over her shoulder to keep an eye on the attacker and also looking forwards at the thrower to watch for the pass, to try to intercept or tip the ball away. Remember the body angle as described in drill 64.

drill 66 *marking relay*

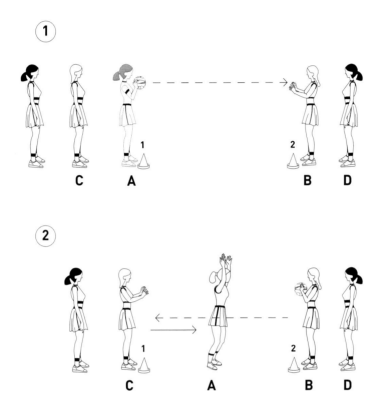

Objective: To practise quick passing and moving to defend the ball.

Equipment: Two cones and one ball between four players.

Description: Place the cones 3–4 m apart. Players A and C start at cone 1. A has the ball. Players B and D start at cone 2. Player A passes the ball to player B using a chest pass and runs to follow the ball, defending the return pass to player C with high arms. Once the second pass is made, player A runs to the back of the line behind player D. Continue until all players have had three runs each, then stop the drill and reaffirm the objectives and key skills.

Coaching points: Look for accurate passes at all times. Encourage players to sprint after the ball and immediately adopt a defending stance with their arms high and fingers spread wide. This will make them as tall as possible, making it hard for the next pass to be thrown accurately.

Progression: Increase the distance between the players and vary the type of pass used.

drill 67 *piggies in the middle*

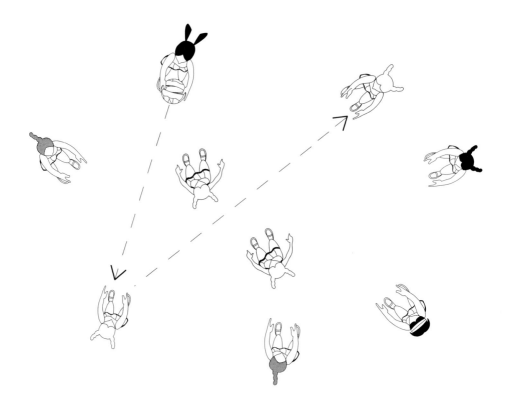

Objective: To develop confidence and quick reactions.

Equipment: One ball between nine players.

Description: Form each group into a circle with two players in the centre. The remaining players pass the ball across the circle using various types of passes. The players in the middle try to intercept the ball. Change players after a certain number of passes have been made. The 'piggies in the middle' keep score of how many touches (1 point), knock-downs (3 points) or catches (10 points) they make. At the end, the player with the most points is the winner.

Coaching points: Look for quick, accurate passes. Defenders should be on their toes, using short, sharp steps to keep moving to intercept.

Progression: Introduce passing without speaking. Receivers signal for the ball (left, right, up, down). Passers can experiment with eye-feints, looking at one player and passing to another, and fake passes.

drill 68 *the triangle*

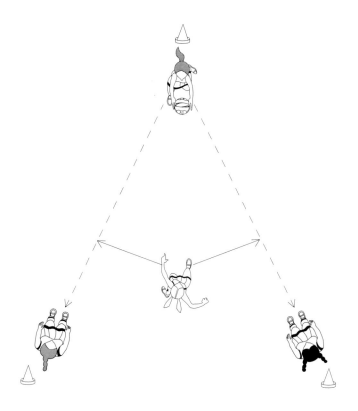

Objective: To practise 'reading' a pass and making the interception.

Equipment: One ball between four players.

Description: Three players stand in a triangle 3–4 m apart. One player, the thrower, starts with the ball. The fourth player is the defender and stands opposite the thrower, between and a little in front of the other two players. The thrower makes a chest pass to either receiver and the defender must try to intercept it. The receiver should land correctly and return the ball to the thrower using a chest pass. Rotate roles after five clean interceptions.

Coaching points: The distance between the players can be varied according to the skill and size of the defender to ensure she has a realistic chance of making the interception. The defender should react to the ball, not to the thrower's eyes. The receivers should make a definite move to get free and receive the pass without contacting the defender. Look for quick, accurate chest passes. Ensure the distance between players is maintained throughout the drill.

Progression: Increase the distance between the receivers.

Objective: To practise timing a run to intercept a pass.

Equipment: One ball between three players.

Description: Players 1 and 2 stand approximately 3 m apart and pass the ball between each other using a chest pass. The defender stands behind player 2 and must run around her to intercept the ball, then returns the ball to the throwers. Rotate roles frequently.

Coaching points: The defender must time her move around the player in order to catch the ball. Look for the defender moving around the player without causing contact and landing in a balanced, controlled way. The defender should move around both sides of the players. Look for good-quality chest passes at all times.

Progression: Vary the type of pass used.

drill 70 *defend the shot*

Objective: To introduce the basic skills of marking a shot for GK and GD.

Equipment: One post, one ball between four players.

Description: GS and GA take it in turns to practise shooting. GK marks GS and GD marks GA to start. In the circle the defender faces the shooting player and tries to make it as difficult for her to make a clean shot as possible by marking the ball with arms outstretched. When the shot has been made all players try to catch any rebound. The ball is passed to the other shooting player and the drill is repeated.

Coaching points: Look for the correct distance from the defending players when marking the shooter to avoid a penalty pass being awarded. Defenders should mark the ball at full stretch making themselves as tall as possible. Encourage the defender to time their move for the rebound as the shot leaves the shooter's hands, and jump to catch the ball. Make sure the defender does not intimidate the shooter by waving her arms in front of her face or shortening the distance between them.

Progression: As players develop their balance and control encourage the defenders to increase their stretch over the ball by standing on one foot and leaning up and over the ball. This is not suitable for younger players who will find it harder to control their balance.

Joanne Harten (England) showing concentration and focus with good shooting technique – essential for successful shooters.

SHOOTING

Shooting is a very specific skill requiring accuracy, good balance, control of movement and confidence in the circle. Most young players want to be goal shooter or goal attack, but players are often complacent in these positions, not fully understanding the complexity of the skills required to be a successful shooter.

A good GS and GA have good awareness of space within the circle and the ability to take control of that space, maintaining focus on a consistent shooting action while under pressure from the defence. For very young players, these are very difficult skills to master. There are some basic drills young players can practise to give them a good understanding of the role of GS and GA, which can be developed as their confidence and experience grow.

In all the shooting drills to follow there are some key coaching points to consider and skills to encourage. The following points are applicable to all shooters; bear in mind it may take some time for younger players to get to grips with them. The height of the post can be lowered to 2 m.

- Young shooters have five seconds to turn and shoot, and the first thing they need to be sure of is correct balance. Feet should be shoulder width apart and toes should be pointing towards the net before a shot is attempted.
- The power and energy for the shot comes from the floor, so the knees should be bent as if the shooter is about to jump into the air. The back should be straight and the head up.
- The ball should be held on the fingertips above the head supported by the other hand, not out in front. The grip should be light, just enough to propel the ball into the net.
- Shooters should focus on a point at the back rather than at the front of the ring, aiming high for the back of the net. This is because if the shot is short it could still fall in!
- Shooters should aim before taking the shot and bend their elbows and knees when ready to shoot.
- The ball should be released at the same time as the shooter straightens her legs. The shooter should move her arms as little as possible, and use a flick of the wrist to add backspin.
- As the shooter prepares to release the ball, she should drop her hands back behind her head. This is the most accurate way to control the direction of the ball.
- The shot should end with the shooter standing on tiptoes with her arms following through towards the ring.

And the golden rule in the circle, for both attackers and defenders: always follow the shot in case it misses – rebounds represent a second chance! Take every opportunity to reaffirm this to form good habits.

drill 71 *shooting skills*

Objective: To introduce and practise the correct shooting action and technique.

Equipment: One post, one ball between two players.

Description: The shooter shoots for goal standing far enough away from the post so as to have a clear aim and not be craning her neck too far. Her partner retrieves the ball and returns it to the shooter using a chest pass. After 10 shots swap roles.

Coaching points: This pass requires balance and control and can be difficult for players to master. Encourage them to think of it as a type of pass – all passes need to be accurate. Look for the correct shooting action – see the introduction to this section. Encourage the shooter to adopt a balanced position and controlled shooting action. The accuracy comes from the balance of the shooter and the timing of the pass combined with the wrist snap and leg push. Encourage the shooter to aim for the back of the ring. Look for a good-quality chest pass from the retriever.

drill 72 *dirty dungeons*

Objective: To practise shooting. This drill works best with older players who have more control of the shooting action.

Equipment: Two balls and two posts.

Description: Divide the players into two teams. Each team has one ball. Each player gets a maximum of one shot per turn. If they are successful with this shot, they stay in the game; if they miss, they must stand in the dungeon (next to the post). Any player standing in the dungeon can be released back into the game by one of their team scoring a goal. Once everybody on one team is in the dungeon the other team wins. For younger players, a target circle on a wall can be used instead of posts. This provides an easier target, but players will still be able to practise a balanced position and the correct shooting action.

Coaching points: Look for correct shooting technique and a balanced position.

Progression: Add a defender to mark the shot.

drill 73 shooting relay

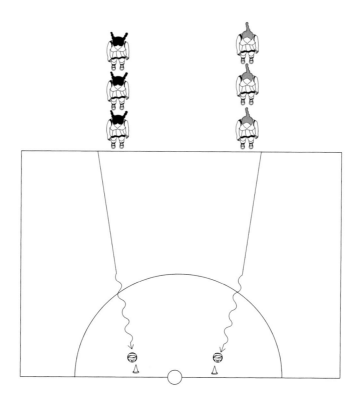

Objective: To practise a balanced shooting position following a move into the circle.

Equipment: Two balls, two cones and one goalpost.

Description: Divide the players into two teams. The balls are placed by the cones on the edge of the circle. Each team starts on a line facing the nearest goalpost. One at a time from each team, players move towards the goalpost using different footwork, such as jogging, skipping or cross-over stepping. The coach or players can decide on the footwork pattern to be used. Once they reach the cone, the players pick up the ball and shoot a goal or have three shots at goal (whichever occurs first), then replace the ball by the cone and run back to the starting line. The next player on their team then begins the drill. Each player needs to complete three trips to the post. The first team to finish is the winner.

Coaching points: Look for balanced, controlled movement into the circle, the correct shooting position and a balanced shooting action.

Progression: With older players, you can add a defender. Alternatively, add a feeder to pass the ball to the shooters as they enter the circle.

Objective: To practise controlling forward movement, getting into a balanced shooting position and maintaining correct shooting action technique.

Equipment: One ball and one goalpost between two players.

Description: One player is shooting, the other is the feeder, standing on the circle edge. The shooter starts on the opposite side of the circle just inside the circle edge, facing the post. When ready, the shooter sprints into the space underneath the post and the feeder passes her the ball. The shooter should jump to catch the ball and land two-footed, then attempt a shot.

Coaching points: Look for a fast, controlled sprint into a space by the shooter and a balanced, two-footed landing. The shooter only has five seconds to shoot once she has received the ball, so the more accurate the pass and the more controlled the landing the better. Look for correct shooting technique and a balanced shooting position.

Progression: Vary the starting positions of the feeder and shooter.

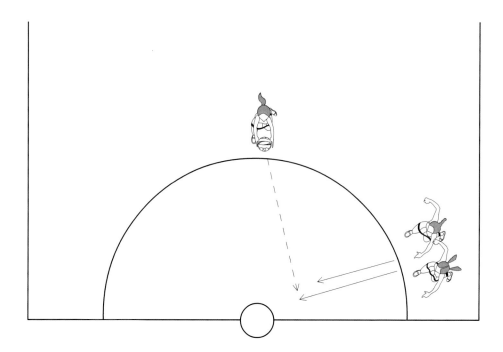

Objective: To practise getting free of a defender to receive the ball under the post.

Equipment: One ball and one goalpost between three players.

Description: Divide the players into groups of three. The feeder stands on the circle edge with the ball. The shooter and defender start opposite the feeder, with the defender between the ball and the shooter. The shooter sprints into the space under the post to receive the ball, aiming to get there before the defender. The defender can try to intercept the ball or tip it to prevent the shooter receiving the ball.

Coaching points: Look for a fast, controlled sprint by the shooter. The defender can hold back at first if the shooter is having difficulty receiving the pass.

Progression: Introduce a dodge for the shooter to get free of the defender and move into a space under the post.

drill 76 *rebound and snatch*

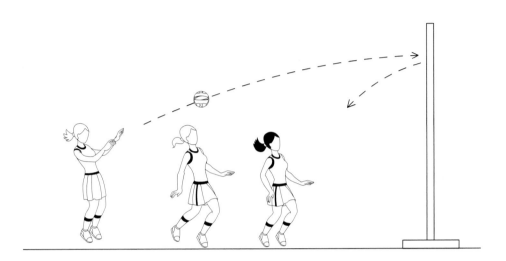

Objective: To encourage young players to chase a loose ball and catch the rebound.

Equipment: One ball and a wall between three players.

Description: Two players are working and one is the feeder. The two working players start facing the wall approximately 2 m away from it. The feeder has the ball and stands slightly behind and to one side of the working players. The feeder throws the ball at the wall, aiming above the heads of the other two players. The working players compete to catch the ball on the rebound, or, if it bounces to retrieve it. A player gets 2 points for catching the ball on the rebound and 1 point if the ball is retrieved after a bounce. Rotate the players after a certain number of throws and compare points at the end of the drill to see who is the winner.

Coaching points: Look for determination to get to the ball first. Watch out for too much contact, but encourage players to snatch the ball to gain possession.

Progression: Use a target circle on the wall for the feeder to aim at.

drill 77 the rebound 1

Objective: To practise following the shot and catching the rebound. This drill is aimed at younger players.

Equipment: One ball and a wall between two players.

Description: Chalk a target circle on the wall approximately 3 m high. One player is the shooter and the other is the defender. They start side by side facing the wall approximately 2 m away from it. The shooter should try to 'shoot' the ball into the target circle, using the correct shooting position and technique. On the rebound, both players should try to catch or retrieve the ball. A player gets 2 points for catching the ball on the rebound and 1 point if the ball is retrieved after a bounce.

Coaching points: Look for the correct shooting technique and position. Players should be determined to get to the ball first. Watch out for too much contact, but encourage players to snatch the ball to gain possession.

Progression: The defender can mark the shooter while she is making the shot and will need to turn to catch the rebound after the shot has been made.

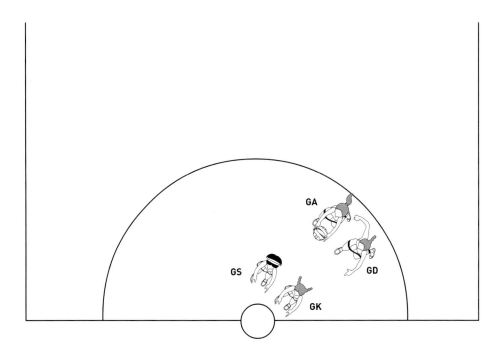

Objective: To practise following the shot and catching the rebound in the circle.

Equipment: One ball and a goalpost between four players.

Description: The GS, GK, GA and GD start in the circle as shown. The shooters take it in turns to take a shot at goal with the defenders marking the shot. The shooter who isn't shooting holds their position under the post waiting for the rebound. The shooter should follow the shot to try and catch the rebound. The defenders should also try for the rebound. Any loose balls should be chased and retrieved. Swap roles frequently.

Coaching points: Look for correct shooting technique and position. The defenders marking the shot will need to turn quickly to try to catch the rebound or retrieve any loose balls. Players should be determined to get to the ball first. Watch out for too much contact but encourage players to snatch the ball to gain possession.

drill 79 *hold that space*

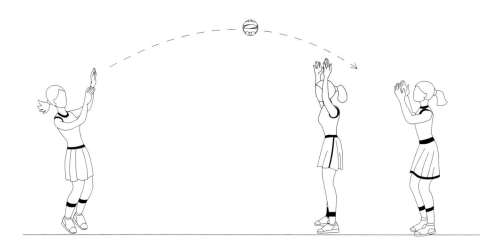

Objective: To practise holding the space behind a player to receive an overhead pass. This can be used under the post or on backline or sideline throw-ins.

Equipment: One ball between three players.

Description: One player is the feeder, one is the attacker and one is the defender. The feeder starts with the ball (this position would be WA, GA or C in a game). The attacker stands behind the defender, slightly sideways, with one foot behind the other, and indicates to receive the ball behind her. The feeder should throw an over-head pass to land behind the attacker, who should hold her position until the ball is overhead and then take one step back to catch the ball.

Coaching points: The attacker should use her body to shield the space in which she wants to receive the ball from the defender. If the attacker moves backwards too early the defender will be able to step back and make an easy interception.

Progression: Vary the position of the feeder so the attacker has to receive the pass from different directions.

GAME SCENARIOS

These drills introduce the basics of a netball game to the younger players, and include the development of quick reactions and decision-making in different game situations, with options for centre passes, throw-ins and attacking and defensive sequences.

Encourage players to try out different positions; this helps them understand the roles and responsibilities of each position and decide which position they prefer or are better suited to, through experience rather than wanting to play a position perceived to be the most popular, i.e. GA or C!

the centre pass

Most young players adopt a very regimented approach to starting the game and the centre pass, standing in the same position on the third line every time, moving the same way and throwing the ball to the same person. The player in the centre position has the pressure of starting the game for her team and often looks to pass to her friend or loudest player on court.

The rule for the start of the game is that all players must be on-side, i.e. standing behind the third line in the attacking or defensive third area with the centre making the pass from the centre circle. It doesn't matter where the GA, WA or GD and WD actually stand in their respective third – in fact as they become more skilled and experienced it is better to keep moving away from their defender before the centre pass is made. This does require confidence and the ability to make quick decisions – a skill younger players need to develop over time.

Aim to keep the practice simple at the start; try and limit the number of things you are asking players to remember. Encourage them to try out different places on the third line when starting the game, to help develop awareness of the options and build the confidence to assert where they want to start the game. This is particularly important if the centre pass isn't going well – starting in a different place can confuse the defender and help make some space to run in to.

Coaching points for young, inexperienced players:

1 Obviously the centre pass is crucial to start the game play and keep possession. Young players often feel a lot of pressure, especially the centre; coaches should stress that all centre court players have responsibility for the centre pass going well. The centre must make a quick decision about who to pass to and make a direct, accurate pass and the WA, GA, GD and WD have the responsibility to get free from their defenders to receive the pass.
2 GA and WA should try to get into position along their third line approximately 3 m from the sideline on the outside of their defender. This gives them space to run in to away from their defender and receive a pass without being blocked in by the sideline.

3 Defenders cannot mark with their arms across the front of the body of their attackers and cannot lean on their attacker.

4 Encourage a straight, direct pass from the centre – a high, looping pass is slower and easier to intercept.

Irene van Dyk of the Silver Ferns jumps for a high pass with Geva Mentor and Sonia Mkoloma of England in defence during the New Zealand v. England match in the New World Series.

drill 80 *whistle ready*

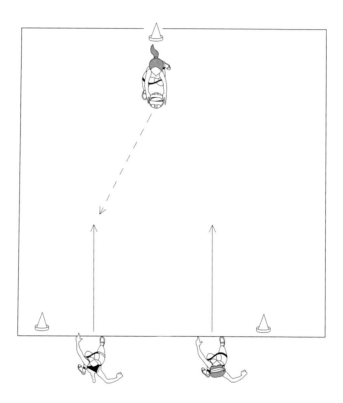

Objective: To introduce and practise the centre-pass movement and improve reactions to the umpire's whistle.

Equipment: One ball and three cones between three players.

Description: Set up players as shown using the cones to mark a triangular working area. The centre starts with the ball. On the coach's whistle, the other two players run in a straight line; the centre must pass the ball to one of the players. Rotate the roles frequently.

Coaching points: Encourage both the centre and the players to react quickly to the whistle as if it were the start of a game. The players must sprint into the space, pushing off on one foot and using their arms to help keep balance and speed. Hands should be ready to receive the ball. The centre should pass the ball into the space the players are running into, not behind them!

drill 81 *attacking centre pass 1*

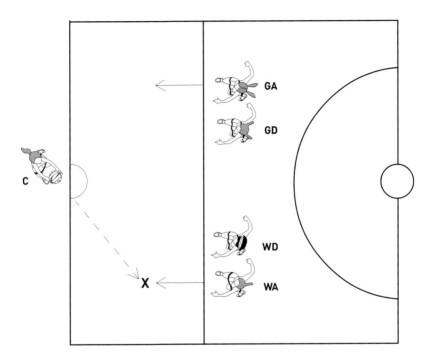

Objective: To introduce and practise attacking centre passes.

Equipment: One ball and half the court between five players.

Description: Set up the players as shown, as if starting a game. The centre pass must go to the WA. On the coach's whistle, the WA runs straight to receive the pass at X. The GA should also run into the centre third as if to receive the pass. The defenders start the drill in position, but should stay still to allow the WA and GA to run into the space easily. The second pass should go to the GA.

Coaching points: The WA should sprint into the space to meet the ball at X. If the WA runs diagonally towards the sideline, she will reduce the space available and make it easier for the WD to intercept the ball. Encourage quick reactions to the whistle.

Progression: The centre can choose who to throw to, WA or GA. The defenders can try to intercept the ball and mark their attacking partner. Encourage older players (WA and GA) to try out different starting points along the line.

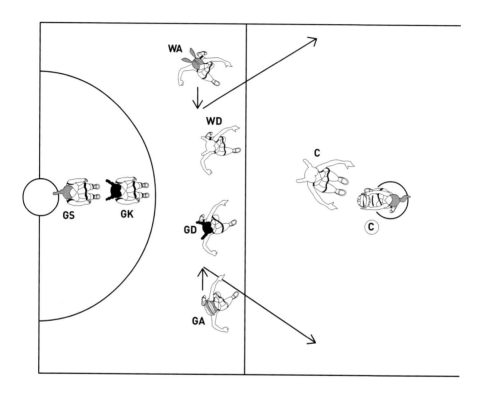

Objective: To practise dodging to get free to receive the centre pass.

Equipment: One ball and half the court between eight players.

Description: This drill provides an alternative way of getting free for the centre pass. On the coach's whistle, the WA and GA dodge to get free and sprint into the centre third. The defenders should stand still at first. The pass can go to either player chosen by the C, but with younger players the coach may need to indicate where the pass should go at first.

Coaching points: The dodge should be a definite movement, controlled, quick and balanced. Look for the WA and GA pushing off on their outside foot and using their shoulders to help perform the dodge and make the move quick and controlled.

Progression: Introduce the defenders. Encourage them to try to stick with their players and intercept the ball.

drill 83 *the centre pass using WD and GD 1*

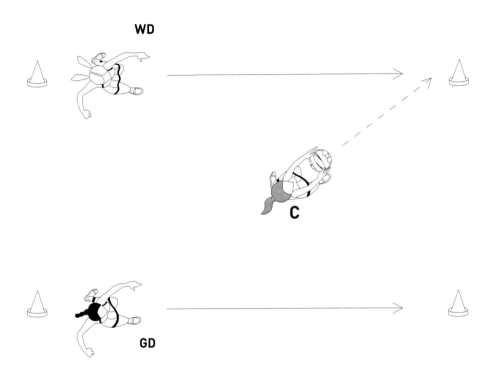

WD

C

GD

Objective: To introduce using the WD and GD to receive the centre pass. This drill is aimed at older, more experienced players.

Equipment: One ball and four cones between three players.

Description: The idea behind this drill is to reproduce the centre court positions at a centre pass for the WD, GD and C. Divide the players into groups of three and use the cones to mark out a working area approximately 5 m square. The C stands in the middle of the square with the ball. The WD and GD start at the cones as shown, standing behind the C. On the coach's whistle the WD and GD sprint in a straight line towards the opposite cones. The C should pass the ball to either player, aiming for them to catch the ball at the cone in front of them.

Coaching points: Look for the WD and GD sprinting towards the second cone. The C must wait for the players to pass her before throwing the ball.

Progression: Introduce a WA and GA to mark the WD and GD. The WA and GA should stand outside the WD and GD, sprinting with them to try to intercept the ball.

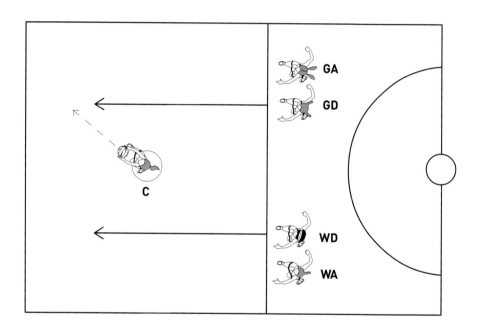

Objective: To practise WD/GD receiving a centre pass in an attacking position.

Equipment: One ball and half the court between five players.

Description: Set up the players as shown. The C starts with the ball and should be facing away from the WD and GD. On the coach's whistle, WD and GD sprint in a straight line, aiming to receive the ball as close to the attacking third line as possible. Alternate the players receiving the pass. Restrict defending players (WA and GA) until the WD and GD are more confident.

Coaching points: To receive a centre pass without a good chance of the ball being intercepted, the WD and GD should position themselves inside their defending players ready for the centre pass. It is worth letting the WD and GD try to receive the centre pass having started on the outside of their defending players; this puts the C under more pressure to make an accurate pass and makes it easier to intercept by the WA and GA.

Progression: Encourage the defending players to try for the interception. Look for the player receiving the pass to make a second pass to either the WA or GA.

the throw-in

The player taking the throw-in depends on where on the court the ball goes out of play. Younger players don't always think about the positioning and spacing on court and are keen to take throw-ins to be part of the game, wherever the throw-in may be. However, if a player taking the throw-in is out of position on the court, it will have an impact on the next sequence of passes in the game. Encouraging young players to think about the 'correct' person to take the throw-in is a good habit to get into.

The following drills enable players to practise set moves for a variety of throw-ins, although the combinations are endless and players will need to be encouraged to be flexible and think about the best options available in each situation.

Coaching points to consider when taking a throw-in

1   The player must stand with one foot up to but not touching the sideline of the court. This indicates to the umpire that the player is ready to make the pass. If the player's feet are touching the line, a free throw-in will be given to the opposite team. An umpire may also penalise a player who is standing too far away from the line – this is not likely to happen with younger players, but good positioning is worth encouraging.
2   The player taking the throw-in should look to pass the ball in to an attacking or forward position on court. There may be occasions when the throw-in will need to be passed backwards if players are not free, but players should be encouraged to look forwards.
3   All players must be on court before the pass is taken. This also applies to members of the opposite team who may have gone off court to retrieve the ball. If a player takes the throw-in without waiting for that player to get back on court, a free pass will be given to the opposite team.
4   Players on court should be ready to receive the pass, either holding a space to run into or ready to dodge and get free.
5   Players defending a throw-in should be 1 m away from the sideline to avoid giving away a penalty pass.
6   Any backline throw-in taken in the defensive goal third should be taken by the GK.
7   Never throw a backline pass across the circle, as if the pass is intercepted it will give the attacking team an immediate shot at goal.

The player taking the throw-in can decide whether to take the throw-in quickly or take more time. There may be an advantage if the throw-in is taken quickly, for example to get the ball into the circle to an unmarked GA or GS. Don't forget to encourage players to make sure all players are on court before the throw-in is taken to avoid a free pass being given to their opponents (see point 3 above). There may also be advantages to taking more time to prepare before taking the throw-in, for example if team players are out of position and need time to recover on court.

This may be too complicated for younger players, who, as we have already mentioned, tend not to think about spacing and timing of passes on court. It is something that coaches can introduce to more experienced young players.

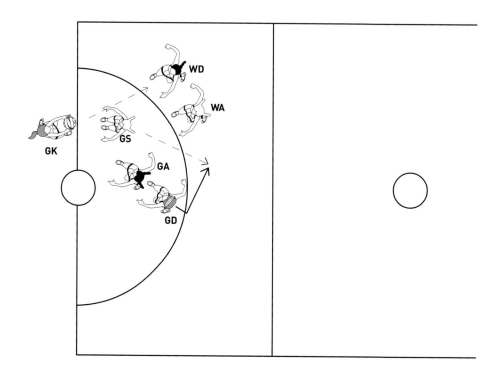

Objective: For the WD and GD to practise receiving a backline throw-in taken in the circle.

Equipment: One ball and one third of the court between five players.

Description: The defensive backline pass is easy in terms of who takes the throw-in, as it will always be the GK wherever the ball goes out of court. The GK starts with the ball standing on the backline. The other players start in the positions as shown above. The WD and GD should hold their positions on the edge of the circle, making it harder for the WA and GA to mark their free side. When ready, the GK should step up to the line as if to take the throw-in. The WD or GD should aim to receive the pass at the edge of the circle, shielding the ball from the WA or GA with their bodies.

Coaching points: Encourage the WD and GD to hold the space on the edge of the circle. Any movement before the pass will give an advantage to the defender.

Progression: The GD or WD should be ready for the next pass.

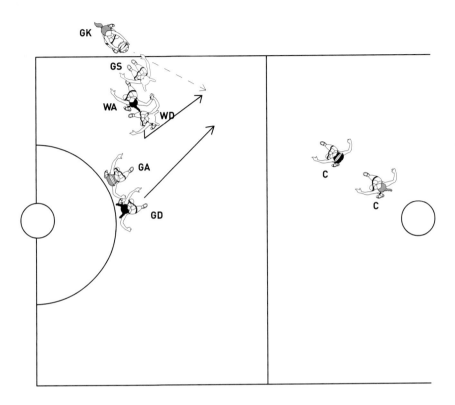

Objective: To practise a sideline throw-in in the defensive third.

Equipment: One ball and one third of the court.

Description: In this situation the GK should take the throw-in. The WD or GD should aim to receive the pass. With younger players, the coach may need to dictate which player should receive the pass and alternate. WD and GD should dodge to get free of their marker or hold a space to run into.

Coaching points: Encourage the players to hold their space and resist moving up the court to help receive the pass, which will cause crowding.

Progression: The GK should decide which player to pass to depending on who is in the best position to receive the pass.

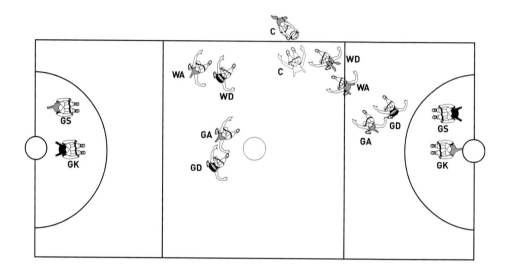

Objective: To practise a throw-in in the centre court. The aim is to encourage players to decide who will receive the throw-in and avoid crowding around the ball.

Equipment: One ball and the whole court.

Description: The coach should vary the position of the throw-in. Let the players play out the sideline pass, aiming to maintain an attacking position.

Coaching points: The coach must ensure that a clear pass is given and that the player receiving the throw-in makes a definite move to receive the ball. The other players should avoid crowding and look to receive the next pass. Encourage lots of communication and stop the drill if players do crowd the ball. Walk them through the moves if needed.

Progression: Vary the player taking the throw-in and receiving the pass. Encourage the players to take responsibility for deciding who will take the throw-in and receive the pass, rather than the coach dictating this all the time.

attacking sequences

The following game scenarios practise attacking sequences working in the centre and goal-shooting third. They concentrate on the role of the attacking players and provide typical set piece situations. Sequences for the defence are covered later.

It is useful for young players to try out all the positions even if they already think they are a born GA. This gives players a better understanding of the different roles in the netball team, the responsibilities of each position and the difficulties faced by each one. Also, unless a player has played a position in a game situation, it is difficult for them to make an informed decision about whether they want to play that position or not. Excellent netballers can play in a variety of positions. Versatility is the key – encourage young players to try different positions and have fun in the process.

Key coaching point

When feeding the ball into the circle, the WA and C should work together aiming to have one player at the top of the circle – see diagram.

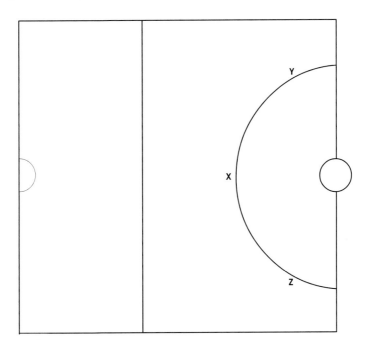

X is the top of the circle – a key attacking position. WA or C should aim to get to the top of the circle which then allows them to pass the ball to either side of the circle or to feed the ball into the shooters.

If C is holding the space at the top of the circle, WA should take up position at Y or Z and vice versa. This gives the attacking team a strong position controlling the space around the circle edge.

drill 88 *to the circle*

Objective: For GA and GS to practise working in the circle together, focusing on space awareness and control of space.

Equipment: One ball and one third of the court between four players.

Description: This drill does not include defenders in order to let the attacking players gain confidence in the use of space in the attacking third. The GS should hold the space under the post while the WA starts with the ball in the centre third as if she has just received a centre pass. The C and WA pass the ball to the circle edge, aiming for one player to reach X and the other Y. The ball should then be fed into the circle to the GA or GS, who should try a shot.

Coaching points: Encourage the players to communicate with each other and make definite moves into space. There should be little hesitation between passes. Stop the sequence if the game breaks down and encourage players to avoid crowding the ball. Shooters should adopt the correct shooting position and use correct technique.

Progression: Aim to get the ball into the circle with the fewest number of passes.

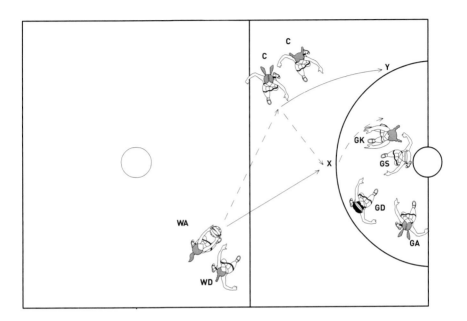

Objective: To introduce GD and GK to the GA and GS working in the circle, getting free to receive a pass and practising awareness and control of space.

Equipment: One ball and the attacking third of the court between eight players.

Description: Defending players should all mark their partners, intercepting passes where possible. GS should hold the space under the post. WA starts with the ball in the centre third, as if a centre pass has just been received. The attacking players pass the ball to reach the circle edge, aiming for one player to reach X and the other Y. The ball should be fed into the circle for the GA or GS to try a shot.

Coaching points: Encourage the attacking players to communicate and make definite moves to get free. Stop the sequence if the game breaks down and constantly encourage players to avoid crowding the ball. If the ball is intercepted, the defenders get 1 point and the drill restarts.

Progression: Aim to get the ball into the circle with the fewest number of passes.

defensive sequences

The following game scenarios provide some basic drills for defenders working in the centre and defensive goal third. They concentrate on the role of the defending players and typical set piece situations.

Remember, versatility is the key – encourage young players to try different positions in defence as well as in attack and have fun in the process.

Key coaching points

1 A defender should always try to catch the ball – if a player can get one hand to a ball to hit it away from the attacker, she could catch the ball and gain possession.
2 All players will need to be able to defend at certain times in a game – it is as important for a WA, GA and GS to be able to defend the ball, defend their space and mark a player as it is for a WD, GD and GK.
3 The first step for young players is to learn how to mark an attacking player, sticking to their opponent like glue to prevent them receiving a pass.
4 When players become more experienced and are more aware of the space on the court, they can then progress to 'defending a space' – preventing an attacking player from moving into a space to receive a pass. Players need to be able to read the game well, anticipating where the next pass will be and moving early to prevent the pass being made.

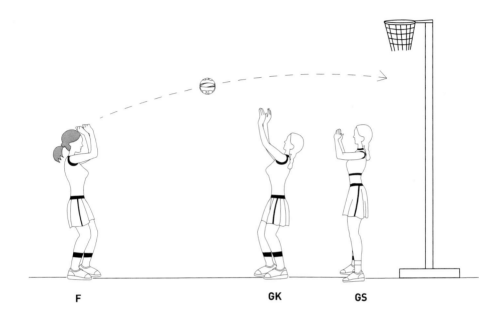

F   GK   GS

Objective: For the GK to practise marking the GS, holding a space under the post.

Equipment: One ball and one post between three players.

Description: Start with the GS and GK under the post and a feeder (F) with the ball outside the circle. The GS aims to receive the ball under the post by holding the space, the feeder throwing an overhead pass into the space. The GK marks the GS closely, giving her as little space to move as possible. The GK should try to jump and intercept or 'tip' the ball off court to prevent the GS from receiving the pass, receiving 1 point if she is successful. The GS should shoot if the pass is successful. The drill restarts if the ball is intercepted or a goal is scored.

Coaching points: The GS should face the feeder. The GK should always be between the ball and the GS; if the GS is in front of the GK this allows an easy pass.

Progression: Vary the position of the feeder.

drill 91 *into the circle*

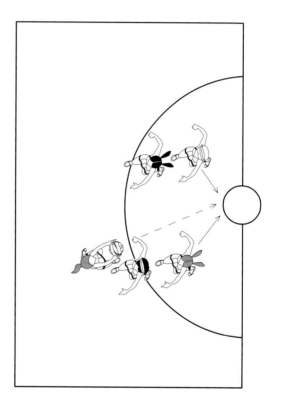

Objective: For GK and GD to practise defending in the circle, and for GS and GA to practise getting free and develop awareness and control of space in the circle.

Equipment: One ball and one post between five players.

Description: GA and GS stand in the circle, defended by the GK and GD. The feeder stands on the edge of the circle. The shooters dodge to get free and indicate where they want to receive the ball. The feeder passes the ball to each shooter in turn. The shooter should then make the shot, following the ball. The second shooter takes control of the space under the post, waiting for the rebound and blocking her defender. The defenders should aim to intercept the ball or get the rebound. Shooters get 1 point for a goal and 2 points for a rebound caught. Defenders get 1 point for an interception and 2 points for a rebound caught.

Coaching points: Look for close marking from the defenders and confidence in movement, dodging into space and holding space from the shooters.

Progression: Vary the position of the feeder.

drill 92 *half game*

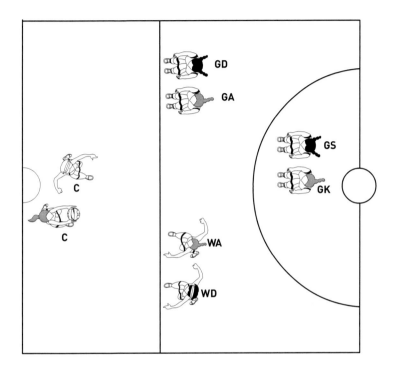

Objective: For players to practise a variety of skills in a game situation.

Equipment: One ball, bibs, half the court between eight players.

Description: Set up a game in half the court to restrict space and allow players to practise specific skills. The coach can apply conditions to the game, for example only chest passes can be used, only WA can receive the centre pass, no passing back to the player from whom you received the ball and so on.

Coaching points: Look for good-quality passes and movement towards the ball to receive a pass. A free pass can be given to the opposite team if a condition is not applied. Check players' understanding of the drill regularly. Any loose ball should be chased.

Pamela Cookey of England and Rebecca Bulley of Australia contest for the ball under the post showing the physical skills and determination needed in netball.

CONDITIONED GAMES

Young players not only have to learn the basic skills of netball (balance, control, passing and catching techniques, footwork etc.), they also have to learn the roles and responsibilities of the seven team positions and be able to understand sufficiently to put all this into practice in a game. This is quite a big ask when players are just starting out and they will need lots of support, encouragement and praise to help them develop these skills.

There can be a tendency for players to revert back to old habits when playing in a game, rather than try newly coached skills or techniques; even if you have just delivered a highly successful coaching session incorporating well-structured drills! When players are under pressure, faced with defenders, and with limited time to choose and make their pass, with teammates calling out for the ball to be passed to them, the easy, safe option is to hurl the ball any which way and get rid of it! The drills they have just run through are long forgotten.

Enthusiasm can often get the better of players too, with everyone running after the ball, shouting at teammates with little regard for positions on the court, spacing and control.

To encourage players (of all ages and abilities!) to practise using the skills you have drilled during coaching sessions in a game situation it sometimes helps to make the new skill or technique a condition in the game, with a failure to use or apply this rule resulting in a free pass to the opponents.

The following drills are suggestions for conditioned games that I have found particularly helpful for young, inexperienced players to help them develop their netballing skills and improve their understanding of the role of the positions and spacing on court.

Coaching points:

1. Link the condition in the game to the drills that have been practised as part of the training session – the idea is to encourage players to try out their new skills.
2. Only apply one condition at a time for young players – don't give them too much extra to think about, this will only confuse things.
3. Use conditioned games for a short time to avoid frustration building when trying to learn something new.
4. Encourage players to spot when the skills and techniques have been used – this is useful for players waiting to join in the game and for players on the court – extra points can be awarded if the team spots when the condition has been correctly applied.

drill 93 *space out!*

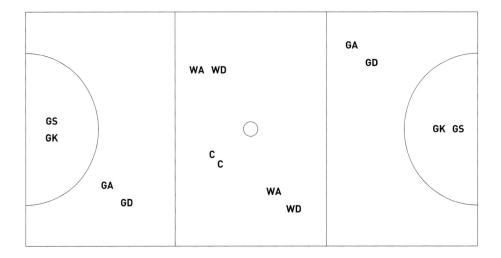

Objective: To encourage players to be more aware of their main area of responsibility and the space on the court. Particularly aimed at GA and GD to prevent them hovering out of position at their opposite third line.

Description: GA and GD on each team are restricted to their goal third and not allowed to move into the centre third to receive a pass apart from the centre pass. The condition of the game is that they must play in the same area as GS and GK.

Coaching points: This helps to keep players evenly spaced throughout the court and prevents the GA or GD being out of position by moving up to her opposite third line when the opposing team are attacking or defending. This means the GA will always be in her attacking third when the ball is being moved into attack – important as she is one of only two shooters! When a backline pass is being taken from the defending team, or following an interception, encourage passes to be made in sequence through the team positions: GK to GD or WD, to C, to WA then GA, as the ball moves up the court towards the circle. Defenders should be making and receiving passes in the defending half, attackers in the attacking half.

drill 94 get free!

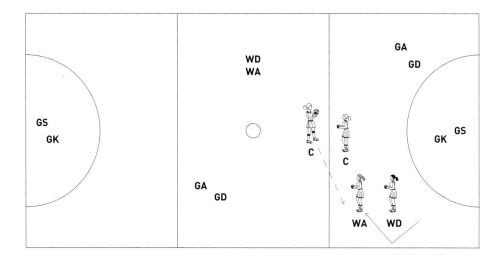

Objective: To encourage players to dodge and get free of their defender to receive a pass.

Description: All passes in a game to be a chest pass.

Coaching points: Remind players that a chest pass is used for short distances and look for good chest passing technique. Encourage players to make a dodge and move forward towards the player with the ball to receive the pass. The condition can be relaxed for passes into the circle – unless you want to encourage the GS and GA to move forward to receive their pass.

drill 95 *make that pass!*

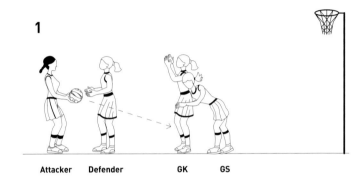

1

Attacker   Defender   GK   GS

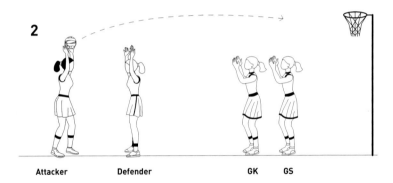

2

Attacker   Defender   GK   GS

Objective: To encourage players to practise a bounce or lob pass into the circle to avoid the defenders.

Description: All passes made into the circle to a GA or GS to be a bounce or lob pass. Pick one pass as the condition for young players – for more experienced players both types of pass can be applied.

Coaching points: Look for good passing technique. For a lob pass encourage the GS and GA to hold their space under the post and stand still, waiting to receive the pass until the ball is overhead. Encourage them to jump to catch the ball out of the air and not to move too soon which will make it easier for the defenders to intercept the ball.

drill 96 arms up!

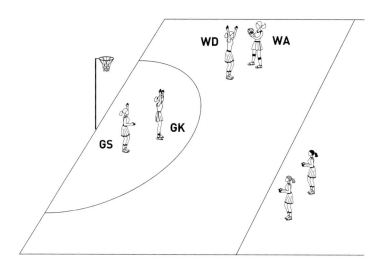

WD   WA

GK

GS

Objective: To encourage players to defend when their opponent has the ball and to increase awareness of when a game situation moves from attack to defence.

Description: Players must mark their players facing towards them with their arms up when their opposing team player has the ball. The aim is for them to make it as difficult as possible for the player to make an accurate pass.

Coaching points: Look for the correct distance when marking the player with the ball, to avoid a penalty pass being awarded. Encourage players to quickly move to defending the ball and encourage teammates to do the same, for example after an interception when one team will be moving from defending to attacking.

WARMING DOWN

At the end of the session the players will be hot and probably tired. It is a mistake to just say, 'Thanks for coming' and let them wander off. Instead, you should always incorporate a warm-down to develop good habits and provide a number of important functions:

- a great opportunity to work on flexibility as the muscles are warm
- allows the body to begin to flush out many of the waste products produced during vigorous exercise
- represents a clear end to the session, ensuring that players feel they have had a well-thought-out, well-structured session, which all adds to the atmosphere of excellence and care that will motivate a group to work effectively.

Just as with all the drills, the warm-down sessions must focus on form; only strict form will provide the intended benefits.

drill 97 *hamstring reach*

Objective: To improve flexibility and warm down the body.

Equipment: One ball per player.

Description: Line the players up along the baseline with their feet over shoulder width apart and the ball between their feet. On the coach's command, the players reach down (keeping their legs straight, but with a slight bend in the knees so the legs are not locked, pick up the ball and place it as far back through their legs as they can. The players then walk backwards until their feet are in line with the ball once more, and repeat the drill. The aim is to cover the given distance (approximately 10 m) in as few pick-ups as possible.

Coaching points: Watch for cheats who bend their legs to gain an advantage. This is a slow, controlled drill and form is everything.

drill 98 *side stretch*

Objective: To improve flexibility.

Equipment: One ball per player.

Description: Line the players up with their right side facing into court, their feet over shoulder width apart, their legs straight and the ball in front of their left foot. On the coach's command, the players bend down (keeping their legs straight), pick up the ball and place it in front of their right foot. Leaving the ball where it is, the players then swap feet, progressing into the court, so that the ball is by their left foot once more. The movement is then repeated for a set distance before the players return to the start; 10 m is more than enough for this drill.

Coaching points: Watch for cheats who bend their legs to gain an advantage.

drill 99 *circle stretch 1*

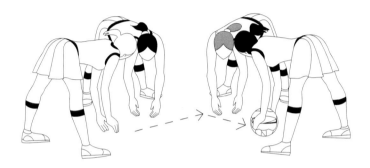

Objective: To improve flexibility.

Equipment: One ball between four players.

Description: Players form a circle with their feet over shoulder width apart and touching the feet of the next players. Keeping their legs straight, the players reach down and hang their hands as close to the floor as possible. The ball is rolled from one player to another around the circle. After 10 passes in total, walk the players around for a minute and then repeat.

Coaching points: Watch for cheats who bend their legs to gain an advantage.

Progression: If you have enough players, form two or more groups and race to see which is the first to complete the passes.

drill 100 *circle stretch 2*

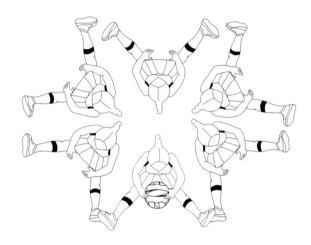

Objective: To improve flexibility.

Equipment: One ball between about six players.

Description: The players sit facing outwards in a circle with their feet wide apart and touching the feet of the next players. The ball is passed in order around the circle. Each player must give and take the ball with two hands every time.

Coaching points: This drill provides a stretch to the backs of the legs and requires good flexibility in order to be able to rotate the trunk and make the pass. If players are short on flexibility they will creep their bottoms away from the group so that they are leaning back rather than sitting upright. Encourage them to keep their legs nice and straight throughout.

Progression: If you have enough players, form two or more groups and see which is first to complete the passes. Vary the direction of the pass on command.

drill 101 *giant strides*

Objective: To improve flexibility.

Equipment: Half the court.

Description: Line the players up facing into court. Keeping the body upright, they should take a slow, controlled stride forwards. The stride should be as large as control will allow. Repeat over a set distance (10 m is fine) and then walk the players back to the start and repeat.

Coaching points: This drill only works if the body is strictly upright with a 'proud' chest and the head up. The more slowly this drill is performed, the better. The challenge is for each player to beat her own score; if they can cover the distance in five strides, they should try to cover it in four and a half next time and so on.